The Agreement

Unlocking the Favor of God

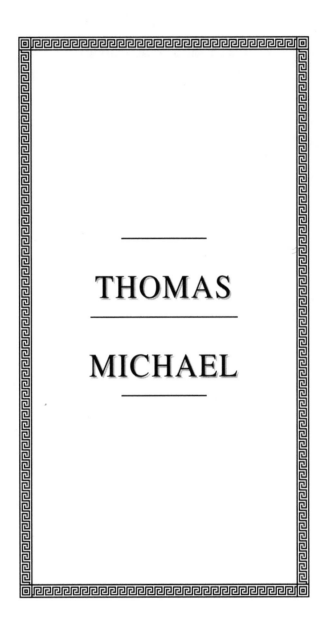

THOMAS

MICHAEL

THE

AGREEMENT

The Agreement

Unlocking the Favor of God

ISBN 0-9703932-3-7
Copyright © 2000
Thomas Michael

Published by:
Falcon Publishing Co.
P.O. Box 200367
Arlington, TX 76006
United States of America

Cover Design by Joe Harrison and Kevin Copeland

Book Production by
Jason Countryman - Pocket-Pak

Falcon Publishing

The Agreement

UNLOCKING THE FAVOR OF GOD

Dedication

To my loving wife, Judy... my partner, my friend, my lover, my soul mate, my desire.
Thank you for staying in the Agreement these past 18 years. Ours is a love truly based on
Agreement and it will last forever.

Acknowledgements:

My precious Power Church family, I cannot imagine life without you. You are my "agreeable factor". To my staff, Michael Callis, Pastors Thomas and Dana DeAndrea, Elizabeth DeLaGarza, Pastor Joel Eason, Blenda Gamez, Pastor Joseph Harrison, Melanie Hart and Jeff Kuhn. Thank you for your love and support.

A special thanks to Drew Carlson who spent many hours transcribing tapes and laying the foundation for the excellence carried out in this work.

To the most anointed assistant, Melanie Hart, you are a God-send. Your endless, tireless support and hard work are recorded in the archives of Heaven. Trina Gamez, thank you for your care to detail; it makes your spirit of excellence shine! To Melanie, Blenda, Trina, Elizabeth and Zina, thank you for the hundreds of hours spent on research. Your honor and respect for me speak volumes of your character.

ponsors:

~Gold Partners~

Tom and Blenda Gamez & June Bunch
Kathy Terry Douglas
Trina Gamez
Melanie Hart
Ann Hill
Rodney and Robin Mallard
Dr. Mike Murdock
Joe and Lorena Rodarte
Ernest and Lidia Ybarbo

~Silver Partners~

Anita-Louise.
Ann J. Collins
Patsy Cowan
David and Geni Douglass
Pastor Joel and Carolee Eason
Raymond and Soledad Edwards
Jeff, Cheryee and Hunter Kuhn
Lyndia Land
Luis and Pam Pereira

TABLE OF CONTENTS

TABLE OF CONTENTS -CONTINUED

He is *trusted*, because of his untarnished *integrity*.
He is *respected*, because of his consistent *prayer life*.
He is *treasured* for his unswerving *loyalty*.
He is *loved* for his genuine compassion for the *hurting*.
He is *celebrated* for his rare musical *genius*.
He is *remembered* for the unforgettable *anointing* he carries.

Now, Pastor Thomas Michael is imparting to the Body of Christ what may become his greatest legacy -- **THE AGREEMENT.** I read this manuscript in the Secret Place, my private place for meeting with the Holy Spirit, daily. Truly, the Spirit has burned this divine and life changing revelation into the heart of this uncommon man of God.

This book could change your *marriage instantly.*
This book could change your *ministry...*forever.
You cannot read this book and remain unchanged.

I've known him as my personal friend...my pastor...my special guest at our Wisdom Conferences. He lives and breathes what he teaches, 24 hours a day. He and his beautiful wife, Judy, have left thousands, almost breathless, through their unforgettable gift of music. Now, I see him planting the incredible Seed that will possibly birth the greatest wave of healing you've ever known in your personal life -- **THE AGREEMENT**.
Get alone. Read this book *aloud*. Keep reading past the controversial insights. (You'll revisit them later with understanding.)
You'll soon understand, clearly, why the Holy Spirit created your divine linkage to this book. Your greatest mysteries will soon become your greatest miracles.

In Agreement,

Mike Murdock
Dr. Mike Murdock

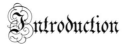

Introduction

In my pastorate, I have seen many people come and go from my church. The majority of those who left were offended when they made their exit, perhaps, because they came to me with offense already resident. My purpose in life is to bring people into the presence of God through worship. However, offense is the enemy of true worship and results in polluted sacrifice to God. I have been commissioned by God to be His Instrument of Worship, and now, He has given me a mandate to take this message around the world.

Agreement is the Essence of the Godhead, because They are One. I pray that the message of unity among the Godhead is conveyed to you in a most precise manner through this book. *The realm of the Spirit is order.* It is my desire for you to come into right order with my Partner of Agreement, the precious Holy Spirit. I am in agreement with you for the increase of revelation knowledge in your life. This book will cause your faith to be complete. *The Fruit of Agreement is Favor.*

In Hebrews 11:3, the word "framed" is the same Greek word used to describe a potter who decides to take his already existing work of clay and change it, completely altering its present shape. The Amplified Bible says: "By faith we understand that the worlds [during the successive ages] were *framed* (fashioned, put in order, and equipped for their intended purpose) by the Word of God, so that what we see was not made out of things which are visible." Everything that we see was made or "framed" from the **Agreement** among the Godhead. The Greek further describes "framed" meaning to complete thoroughly, perfectly joined together, prepare, restore, touching, beyond measure, perfect, bear up and lift up. My paraphrase of this verse: *Through faith we recognize that different time periods, different decades, centuries, millenniums, different generations within the past history of mankind have been brought to completion; thoroughly, perfectly joined together, prepared, restored, touched, beyond measure, perfected, and lifted up by the Agreement of the Word of God.*

May God give you a divine revelation of His Agreement through the pages of this book. When you have experienced the Anointing of Agreement, you will have reached the apex of human experiences. It is the revelation of the Father, the Son, and the Holy Ghost, the Agreed Godhead.

Thomas Michael

~1~

THE POWER OF AGREEMENT

Power Key: *Agreement Is A Discovery.*

ong before there was time…
Before anything was made that was made…
Before existence existed, there were Three yet One.

They abode together in Absolute Agreement.

In the atmosphere of perfect, supreme, uncontaminated, undefiled unity…

In the aura of sovereignty, equanimity, sequence, balance, and order…

From this pristine environment came forth the essence of the Godhead; **The Agreement.**

John 1:1-5(KJV), In the beginning was the Word, and the Word was with God, and the Word was God. The same was in the beginning with God. All things were made by him; and without him was not anything made that was made. In him was life; and the life was the light of men. And the light shineth in darkness and the darkness comprehended it not.

~If Any Two Shall Agree~

Matthew 18:19, Again I tell you, if two of you on earth **agree** *(harmonize together, make a symphony together) about whatever [anything and everything] they may ask, it will come to pass and be done for them by My Father in Heaven.*

Late one Saturday night, I sat in my study searching the Scriptures for a message to share with my congregation the following morning. As any caring pastor, I was looking for something my sheep could feast on. Never in my wildest imagination did I dream that God would reveal a mystery that would change my life forever.

I cannot tell you how many times I have read Matthew 18:19. I have probably quoted it a thousand times since receiving Christ in my early childhood years. I have recited it to my congregation and in prayer when ministering to people. It is a wonderful verse to claim.

This time the verse exploded in my spirit. I had just completed a revelatory teaching series entitled: **Offense: The Secret Power of Lawlessness.** The topic of offenses was fresh in my mind and spirit. Upon reading the phrase, *If any two shall agree...*I was quickened by the Holy Spirit that the little word **"agree"** was the annulment of offense. I recognized **Agreement** as the very thing that would undo offenses.

What an astonishing statement! If two or more persons simply *agree* on *anything*, the Father Himself *will do it* for them. This was too good to be true. Nevertheless, there it was in biblical black and white, stated by the Lord Jesus Himself.

I had often wondered why so many believers suffer when the Bible promises *a life more abundant.* I came to understand the condition for the promise in this passage was *agreement with one another*, a simple concept, yet profound.

On the other hand, is it?

As I studied that night and in the subsequent months, I came to realize biblical agreement is much, much more than a polite *spiritual handshake* with another believer during prayer. Agreement is not formulaic. Quite frankly, it is more than the futile prosperity gospel often preached in parts of the Church today. The blessings promised in Matthew 18:19 are not released by *"naming it and claiming it"* or *"blabbing it and grabbing it."*

Biblical agreement operates at a much more profound level, demanding deep change and commitment from its participants. To enter into agreement with another – to truly *agree* with them – requires complete submissiveness and a forsaking of one's own desires. *The very nature of salvation is rooted in agreement.* It is a contractual agreement between man and God. The whole of Christianity is anchored and firmly established upon agreement. It will become quite evident, as you read in the subsequent chapters, how true that statement really is. Without agreement, Jesus would not have died on

Calvary. He agreed with the Father and gave His life. The word *nevertheless* in Christ's monologue when in the garden of Gethsemane was characteristic of His agreeable nature. The Church would have missed the gift of the precious Holy Spirit if not for the agreement among the one hundred and twenty, who waited in the Upper Room. *The good life is all about agreement!* Agreement is tapping into a new level of humility through worship that unlocks the mercy and the favor of God.

The greatest discovery of my life is the Power of Agreement. As I mentioned in the beginning of this chapter, agreement was present before anything else existed. Before your faith could take shape and form itself, it was an agreement. It was a covenant between you and God. Your faith is completely and totally rooted in agreement. Without agreement, or unity, or whatever word you choose to describe your connection with God, you have no faith. Your belief system is futile without the understanding of agreement.

I have heard many ministers say that every believer will at some point or another go through a period of agnosticism. I have had great difficulty with that statement in times past, being a "faith man". However, when I came to a place in my life when my wife's life depended on "my faith", I can honestly say I did not have confidence of the outcome. What I did have, and have never wavered in, was God's Word. The knowledge of the Word of God sustained me when "my faith" failed me.

~*Knowing, Not "Faithing"*~

The teaching on agreement will unlock the under-standing of synchronizing your life with the Holy Spirit through agreement with His Word and moving into a "knowing" instead of a "faithing". I have often heard people say, "Faith it 'till you make it." Instead, they need to agree and stay in the agreement, "till they make it." Am I saying that you do not need your faith when you are in agreement? No.

Faith is not the significant difference between Christians and the world. There are unsaved people who believe with all their hearts that God is Who He says He is, but they have no relationship with Him. That is because they have not entered into an ***agreement*** with Christ.

It is clear from the Scriptures what pleases God. "Without faith it is impossible to please God..." The Greek word for the word "faith" as found in Hebrews 11:6 means: *to convince (by argument, true or false), by analogy, to rely (by inward certainty):* ***agree***, *assure, believe, have confidence, make friend, obey, persuade, trust, yield.* There is something that pains God more than doubting him; it is the absence of agreement. Hebrews 11:6 could be more appropriately stated:

But without faith...
Without agreement, it is impossible to please God...
Without assurance, belief, confidence...
Without friendship with God...
Without trusting and yielding...

How do you trust what you cannot see? You do not. You trust what you **know**. It is agreement with the **knowledge** of the Word of God that will cause the unseen to become seen.

Faith can never give you assurance of the "seen." Faith is strictly for the unseen. Your understanding and comprehension of the Word is the foundation for your faith. When you know the Word, you do not believe for something "unknown." During the moments when my wife was on her deathbed and my faith could not be found, when I did not know for sure if God could heal her sickness, I knew His Word. God's Word is true and forever settled in Heaven. Agreement with the Word healed my wife when my faith went out the window.

If you stay in agreement with the Word, *"you shall ask what you will and it will be granted to you."*

~Giving To Get~

In today's culture, agreement often carries a "50-50" implication; I will scratch your back if you will scratch mine. For example, you agree with an employer to perform certain tasks every day. The employer agrees to pay you a certain wage. A banker agrees to lend you money to buy a car; you agree to pay it back with interest over 48 months. You agree to vacuum the carpet if your spouse will agree to do the dishes. In the world's system, agreement equates to: I give, you give; we both get.

Nevertheless, in God's inverted kingdom, agreement equates to: "I give, you get." The word **agree** in my computer's thesaurus matched these synonyms: *accede, permit, allow, assent, concede, acquiesce, consent, yield and submit.* Not much "scratch my back, I'll scratch yours" philosophy in those words! Those words are all about **submission** and **not** getting one's own way.

No one who reads the Bible even casually can miss glimpsing God's astonishing love for all people. The Bible boldly declares God's ardent desire to pour out blessings on His children. However, you must understand, although God's **love** is unconditional, His **blessings** are always linked to a condition.

Power Key: *Agreement Is The Requirement For Answered Prayer.*

This is why prayers are not always answered. You routinely **do not** lay down your dreams to make someone else's dreams happen. You worry about **your** goals, **your** finances and **your** fulfillment with scarcely a thought for the dreams of the people in your life. *Agreement means embracing, in every encounter, whatever is best for the other person.*

Agreement does not mean you become a doormat and allow people to walk all over you. It means flowing in the mighty river of love and power that has existed in Heaven for all eternity. To enter into agreement on earth is to tap into the essence of the Father, the Son and the Holy Spirit in Heaven.

Power Key: *Agreement Is The Essence Of The Trinity Because They Are One.*

Agreement is the glue that binds Father, Son and Holy Spirit together. You may have read in I John 4:8 how God is Love. God is also Agreement.

For all eternity, the Trinity has flowed in perfect harmony and humility. Never has there been an argument or outburst of pride between Them. They operate in unending love and submissiveness toward One Another. The members of the Trinity know One Another's minds and thoughts perfectly, and exist in total love, humility and meekness.

Hard to imagine, is it not? Most people cannot go an hour without feeling disagreeable about something, much less an eternity! Husbands, wives, and close friends sometimes taste this phenomenon. They know each other so intimately they can finish one another's sentences and anticipate the smallest of needs.

Power Key: *The Agreeable Person Is A Humble Person, And The Humble Person Is A Powerful Person.*

It may seem odd, even somewhat sacrilegious, to imagine the almighty Trinity existing in humility and submissiveness One with the Other. Consider what Jesus said in the only place in the Bible where He describes His personality. *Matthew 11:29 (KJV), Take My yoke upon you and learn of Me, for I am gentle and lowly of heart, and you will find rest for your souls.* Another version renders Jesus as "meek" and "lowly." According to Strong's Exhaustive Concordance, *tapeinos*, the Greek word for lowly, literally means "low to the ground".

Metaphorically, the word signifies low estate, lowly in position and power, humble.

Power Key: *Agreement Necessitates Humility.*

The almighty Maker of Heaven and Earth described Himself as meek and humble of heart. If you have read the Gospels, you know Jesus was no wimp. With a word, He cast demons out of tormented people. He quieted fierce winds with a simple "Be still." He cleared crooked traders out of the temple with a whip. He went "eyeball to eyeball" with hate-filled, religious leaders who wanted Him dead. He willingly endured a barbaric death on the Cross.

Jesus exuded power accompanied with humility. Meekness and humility are the opposites of pride. Such a combination of character traits might seem odd, even a handicap, in our "can do" culture. Nevertheless, they were the very essence of Jesus when He walked on earth. They are the very essence of Jesus today as He resides with the Father and Holy Spirit.

The agreeable person, then, is of humble character, and the humble person is a powerful person.

~*Agreement And Physics*~

Agreement is being at the right place at the right time, all the time. When you are in agreement, you are in right order - right balance. The principles of agreement, order, and the balance of everything in the universe are founded on Jesus.

Jesus made everything that was made. He was able to defy the law of strong nuclear force, and flowed in agreement with the laws of physics. This is the reason why one should pray in the Name of the Father, and of the Son and of the Holy Ghost. Jesus attached such an amazing promise – *"anything that you ask will be done for you"* – to agreement. He knew first-hand the awesome power inherent in humility. He knew that humility taps into the essence that is the Holy Trinity, unleashing the love and power of God.

Agreement releases the same kind of power Jesus walked in when He was on the earth. Anyone who can walk through stone walls must have a different kind of power working for Him. Jesus operated in a realm of utter agreement with the molecular structure of our three dimensional world, and was able to walk through walls.

As my friend Dr. Vincent Mammarelli, a Spirit-filled scientist in New Jersey, says, "Absolute Agreement is like sharing the same electrons with the Holy Spirit." A covalent bond occurs when two atoms share the same electrons. The same principle applies to our relationship with the Holy Ghost. When there is a total, absolute, unequivocal agreement, the Holy Spirit may enter.

You are probably thinking I have fallen off into the Twilight Zone, more like the Holy Spirit Zone. The absence of offense is the entry to sharing electrons with the Holy Spirit. That, my friend, is agreement! As strange as that may sound, that is what God is requiring before He can release revival on the earth.

The early Church learned this lesson well. In Acts 1:14, they all came into one accord; then in Acts 2:1-4, the Holy Spirit was deposited into the lives of 120 people who waited in agreement. The Power of Agreement created an atmosphere that was conducive for the Third Person of the Godhead, the Holy Spirit, to manifest His power. It is because of the power of agreement that the Holy Spirit was revealed.

~The Time Is Coming~

*Habakkuk 2:14, But [**the time is coming when**] the earth shall be filled with the knowledge of the **glory** of the Lord as the waters cover the sea.*

There is a level of glory God has promised He would pour out upon the earth. This level of glory comes only through pure, undefiled worship. Jesus confirmed this level of glory in the Book of John: *"Jesus said to her, Woman, believe me, **a time is coming when** you will worship the Father neither [merely] in this mountain nor [merely] in Jerusalem. You Samaritans do not know what you are worshiping [you worship what you do not **comprehend**]. We do know what we are worshiping [we worship what we have **knowledge of and understand**], for [after all] salvation comes from [among] the Jews. A time will come, however, indeed it is already here, when the true [genuine] worshipers will worship the Father in spirit and in truth (reality); for the Father is seeking just such people as these as His worshipers. God is a Spirit (a spiritual Being) and those who worship Him must worship Him in **spirit** and **in truth (reality)**."*

The kind of worship the Father desires from His people is from within one's spirit and from the knowledge of the truth. Habakkuk speaks of a time when the **knowledge** of the glory of the Lord covers the earth. We are living in the age of wisdom. There are more Christian books available today than ever before. Yet, man fails to recognize that the Word is dead without the glory. According to Hebrew translation, the ***glory*** means *copiousness, splendor, numerous, rich, honorable, noble, abounding with. **This is where the favor of God is located. It is wrapped in His glory.*** God's dream was to have a people who would worship Him in spirit and in truth (reality) through song. Therefore, He designed the earth to be habitable, unlike any other planet. God strategically placed mankind at the proper place for the purpose of worship. Moreover, His heart still yearns and cries for worshippers that will worship Him in spirit and in truth. Believers know the truth, but few choose to walk in it.

I am confident when the Church grasps hold of the teaching on agreement, it will then fulfill what the prophet Daniel foretold, "The people who know their God shall do mighty exploits."

Acts 2:46, And day after day they regularly assembled in the temple with united purpose...

Acts 4:24a, ...they lifted up their voices together with one united mind to God...

The sense of unity is inescapable in these passages; they are the foundation for the power of agreement. The early Church was immersed in the anointing of agreement.

According to Strong's Exhaustive Concordance of the Bible, *homothumadon*, the Greek term for "with one accord" means: "Being unanimous, having mutual consent, being in agreement, having group unity, having one mind and purpose." In each of its biblical occurrences, *homothumodes* shows a harmony leading to action.

Power Key: *Action And Increase Always Follow Agreement.*

The Greek words for "agree" are *sum* which means together and *phoneo* which means to sound. According to Strong's, the resulting *sumphoneo* means to sound together, to be in accord and harmony. This is where true worship music is born, in agreement.

An agreement must go beyond the initial contract. It is an ongoing, unseen, binding transaction. It is not enough to pray the prayer of agreement with the man of God and then criticize him. The minute you become offended with him, you have breached the agreement. Two believers can walk side by side with each other, but if their hearts are not knit together, they are simply out for a casual stroll.

Power Key: *The Act Of Agreement Is Laying Down One's Dreams and Embracing The Dreams Of Another.*

Matthew 16:24, Then Jesus said to His disciples, if anyone desires to be My disciple, let him deny himself [disregard, lose sight of, and forget himself and his own interest] and take up his cross and follow me [cleave steadfastly to Me, conform wholly to My example in living and, if need be, in dying, also].

The cornerstone of this entire teaching is wrapped up in this passage. Lay down your dreams, enter into covenant agreement with Christ, take up your cross and follow Him. This is the passage way to everything the Father has for you. My Power Key says it this way: *The act of agreement is laying down one's dreams and embracing the dreams of another.*

~Agreement Is A Lifestyle~

Jesus walked side by side with His disciples and yet, disagreement was present. Not everyone who walked with Jesus was able to recognize His deity. Those who did were empowered to remain faithful to the agreement. Peter moved into a close relationship with Christ through the power of the Holy Spirit. It was then the Holy Spirit revealed to Peter the fact that Jesus was the Son of the Living God. That created an intimate relationship between Christ and Peter. When you become intimate with Christ, He is obligated to fulfill the covenant.

Power Key: *Agreement With Man Is Fraught With Failure, But Agreement With God Cannot Fail.*

Agreement is more than a verbal consent; it is a lifestyle. The Church must choose to live in agreement with one another in accordance with the blood covenant agreement of Christ. The operative word in this sentence is *"live"*. Agreement is not based on your emotional stability – it requires the consistency of choice.

The agreement of the first believers created a symphony of worship to God, a harmony that ushered in the birth of the Church. The harmony and submission of a relatively small handful of men and women opened the door for the greatest move of God in history. Just as the agreement of intimacy between a husband and wife brings about new life, so the Church was birthed through the intimacy of agreement.

Something is born every time there is intimacy. Agreement requires intimacy. A businessman cannot enter a contractual agreement with another unless he has had opportunity to have some form of intimate fellowship. Why do you suppose most business deals are sealed over lunch and dinner?

Power Key: *Intimacy Is The Power Of Creation.*

Because the Church was born of agreement, should it not continue in the same unity? The passion in Jesus' "high priestly prayer," found in John 17, relates His mindset just before His death. In a sense, you could say it was His "last wish" even in the midst of His agony on the Cross. However, His real torture ensued when the agreeing Partners of the Godhead were disjoined from Him. Jesus shouldered the offenses of the world alone. The agony of defeat was never preeminent in Jesus' mind; instead, His will, care and devotion were bent on us, His Church and our marriage - our agreement. Try to imagine for a moment the despair that Jesus felt while He interceded for you and prayed: *John 17:11b, 21(KJV),...Holy Father, keep through Thine own name*

*those whom thou hast given Me, that they may be one, as We are. That they all may be **one**; as Thou, Father, art in Me, and I in Thee, that they also may be **one** in Us: that the world may believe that Thou hast sent Me.*

Jesus was prophetically releasing the power and Anointing of Agreement. When Jesus speaks of oneness, He speaks of agreement. He was unlocking the door to salvation.

The unity between Jesus and the Father was the catalyst for the world to believe that He was sent. He alighted upon a society filled with religious people who had long been awaiting their Messiah. Yet, they knew not in which manner He would come. It is evident they were looking for a Messiah who would make His grand entrance with all the pomp and circumstance of an earth-ly king.

They missed their Messiah and nailed Him to a tree. *Five* times Jesus asks the Father to make us "one". If the final supplication of Jesus to His beloved Father was anxiously intertwined and saturated with agreement, should not His people be listening with utmost attentive-ness?

Paul pleads with like intensity in Philippians 2:2 (KJV), when he writes to the church . . .*fulfill my joy by being like-minded, having the same love, being of one accord, of one mind.*

We ignore these impassioned pleas to our great peril. Strife and disagreement continue to rip Christian fellowships, friendships, and churches apart at an unprecedented rate. Divorce is no longer a plague to the heathen alone; it has established itself as an imperious authority in the house of God. It dictates the destiny of so many, as they march in cadence to the pulsation of its commands. Like slaves, oblivious to their destination, they row to the crack of a whip.

Power Key: *Divorce Is The Repugnant Act Of Covenant Breaking.*

A bewitchment much like the foolish Galatians in the New Testament plagues the Body of Christ today. Divorce is not only a problem among the married, it moves like an angel of death through relationships killing off the offspring of the godly. *Divorce is the cause for the spiritual abortion of the unseen.* We may never know or be able to assess the damage of the things that have been lost to *divorcement.* How many dreams and visions have been lost to broken covenant? When will the annihilation of the unseen end? Churches have fallen, futures have been twisted, mangled and redirected with unfortunate ends.

Psalm 15, in one translation, qualifies who may ascend into the holy hill of the Lord. "Anyone who leads a blameless life, and one who keeps a promise even if it ruins him..."; the individual whose focus is pure worship may ascend the hill of the Lord.

Power Key: *Access To God's Presence Outside Of Worship Is Illegal.*

Man's affinity towards the divine has always prompted a desire to access the supernatural. Accessing

God's presence outside of worship is illegal entry to the supernatural.

~Agreement Builds A High-rise~

The people in the Old Testament desired to build a tower that connected them with the heavenlies. The discourse of some theologians is that the Babylonians built their tower with the idea of housing the signs of the zodiac on the top floor. Even with their baneful, distorted ways, their unity and mindset of agreement provided a super ability and their high-rise of enchantment rose to the skies. Impressed by their ability to overlook offense and diversities, God spoke to His Partners in the Trinity and declared in *Genesis 11:6,7, And the Lord said, Behold, they are one people and they have all one language; and this is only the beginning of what they will do, and now nothing they have imagined they can do will be impossible for them. Come, let Us go down and there confound (mix up, confuse) their language, that they may not understand one another's speech.*

When confusion enters the sanctity of relationship, it can transform two intelligent, consenting adults into babbling idiots. Nothing birthed without the consent of the Creator can withstand His fury when He decides its end must come. What man has put together, God can choose to put asunder. God is a merciful God and will allow man to take things to the limit, but He decides the limit.

God is not the author of confusion; He is a God of order. His expectations of man are spelled out in His

Agreement – His Word. *Psalms 138:2, I will worship toward Your holy temple and praise Your name for Your lovingkindness and for Your truth and faithfulness; for You have exalted above all else Your name and Your word and You have magnified Your word [Your Agreement] above all Your name! (Brackets added)* God is going to stand behind His Word – His Agreement, even beyond the power of His Name. God is the God of Covenant and He will stand behind His Word. The only thing that makes the Word of God of none effect is the enemy called hypocrisy. (See Matthew 15:6-9)

Power Key: *Hypocrisy Is The Countenance Of Pride.*

The pride of self-righteousness is the neutralizer of God's Word. Without the effect of God's Word and its boundaries in your life, you easily move into offense.

Power Key: *Offense Is The Enemy Of Agreement.*

Why? What is the enemy of agreement? Sorry, it is not the devil. Deceptive and malevolent as Satan is, the blame cannot be placed on him. No, the blame lies solely within the sanctuary of the saints. As that all wise cartoon philosopher, Pogo, so aptly said, "We have met the enemy, and he is us."

The enemy of agreement is offense. The enemy of God is offense. It is time to get back to God's original intent for His people, a people and a God together free from offense.

~Agreement, The Foundation Of The Church~

The foundation of the New Testament Church was instituted in the upper room when the Holy Spirit moved in response to their Absolute Agreement. This substantiates and gives credibility to agreement as the foundation of the Church. It was founded on the agreement and the unity among the 120 gathered in the upper room.

A person may not enter into the faith of the Gospel without first agreeing with the Word. Then faith is activated: *faith cometh by hearing and hearing by the **Word** of God.* The Word of God is instruction; it is a Testament, an Agreement, a Contract.

Power Key: *Agreement Activates Faith.*

Faith follows agreement. You must first agree with the Word and then your faith is activated. *Hebrews 11:6, But without faith it is impossible to please and be satisfactory to Him. For whoever would come near to God must [necessarily] **believe** that God exists and that He is the Rewarder of those who earnestly and diligently seek Him [out].* The word *believe* in the Greek means: **commit to trust, agree, have confidence, make friend, obey and yield.**

Power Key: *The Realm Of The Spirit Is Order.*

There is no mistaking, God's original order and design for the foundation of the Church was *Agreement*. You must first agree before you can believe! You cannot truly believe that God can heal your relationships unless you first agree. *If any two shall agree as touching anything...* If you agree, then faith is activated and God moves on your behalf! *...it shall be done of our Father who is in heaven.*

You cannot activate anything in the Spirit realm without faith. Hebrews 11:6 says, *"Without faith it is impossible to **please** God..." **Please*** meaning to be fully agreeable, gratify entirely, well pleasing with exciting emotion. What could be more pleasing to God than for His children to walk together in unity? This is the realm of the Spirit called order.

How many Christians do you know that are truly excited about pleasing God? Probably not too many. The division in the Church is not visible on the outside; it is hidden within the hearts of men. Ask the Holy Spirit to reveal any hidden, wrong motives, sins, or breached agreements in your life. You may think that you have not breached an agreement, because you have not walked away from your divinely appointed relationships. Maybe, you are still in the relationship, but perhaps, you have violated one of the five elements of the agreement.

Hidden within every covenant is the objective, the pledge, the instruction, the obligation and the rewards of agreement. Each one of these elements must be upheld.

~The Five Elements Of Agreement~

In every agreement are found the elements that establish the order and authority of the agreement. The five elements of covenant must all be present for an agreement to be valid. The activation of these elements is essential in the efficacy of any agreement.

Allow me to demonstrate the application of the elements of a valid agreement. In the case of Noah's agreement, as outlined in Chapter Nine, it is evident that every "i" was dotted and every "t" crossed.

~1st Element – The Objective~

The first element of God's covenant with Noah is the agreement itself. Every agreement must first begin with a clear picture of the objective. The understanding of the agreeable factor is enveloped within the clarity of the objective.

Genesis 9:8-11, Then God spoke to Noah and his sons with him, saying, Behold, I establish My covenant or pledge with you and with your descendants after you and with every living creature that is with you – whether the birds, the livestock, or the wild beasts of the earth along with you, as many as came out of the ark – every animal of the earth. I will establish My covenant or pledge with you: never again shall all flesh be cut off by the waters of a flood; neither shall there ever again be a flood to destroy the earth and make it corrupt.

An agreement with God is as sure as the rainbow you see on a misty day. My wife and I saw a double rainbow the other day. I suppose, God was just letting us know how faithful He is. Agreement should be like a rainbow. It has all the colors of the spectrum, giving life a little pizzazz.

According to Strong's Concordance, agreement in the Greek means **completeness**. A spiritual agreement necessitates that all the elements work together to bring an agreement to completion.

~2nd Element – The Promise~

Equally as important as the agreement itself is the promise. An agreement without the promise would be deception at its grandest form. *Never enter into agreement with anyone who gives no promise of reward.*

~3rd Element – The Ratification~

The third element of an agreement is the ratification. According to the Webster's dictionary, to ratify something is to give an official sanction, to approve or to confirm. God demonstrated His approval of Noah's agreement with the confirmation of the beautiful rainbow in the sky. The rainbow was a confirmation which provided stability and steadfastness; it created surefootedness for the agreement. *The rainbow was agreement made visible.*

~4th Element – The Obligation~

An agreement would be worthless without an obligatory clause. This is the portion of an agreement that requires determination. You must decide up front whether or not the obligation is acceptable to you and whether or not you are willing to obligate yourself to the agreement. This is the "legally binding" part of the covenant which maintains its validity.

~5th Element – The Fulfillment~

Finally, the fulfillment of an agreement is the manifestation of what has been promised. Few venture this far in the process, due to the escape clause called offense. *Offense is the enemy of agreement.* The only thing that can cause you to breach your agreement is violating the obligation. God is bound to His Word. Even when you feel disqualified to carry on with the agreement, God is merciful and keeps His Word on your behalf.

The agreement is available to every believer who by faith agrees to its conditions and obligations. One can appropriate the benefits of the promise by this vehicle. Every agreement provides a benefit for both agreeing parties, thus giving reason for entering into covenant.

The Scriptures abound with detailed accounts of God's agreement with man. In the case of Adam, God required him to fulfill the obligation; Noah on the other hand received the promise because God bound himself to His Word.

POWER KEYS:

~Agreement Is A Discovery.
~Agreement Is The Requirement For Answered Prayer.
~Agreement Is The Essence Of The Trinity Because

They Are One.
~The Agreeable Person Is A Humble Person And The
Humble Person Is A Powerful Person.
~Agreement Necessitates Humility.
~Action And Increase Always Follow Agreement.
~The Act Of Agreement Is Laying Down One's Dreams
And Embracing The Dreams Of Another.
~Agreement With Man Is Fraught With Failure, But
Agreement With God Cannot Fail.
~Intimacy Is The Power Of Creation.
~Divorce Is The Repugnant Act Of Covenant Breaking.
~Access To God's Presence OutsideOf Worship Is Illegal.
~Hypocrisy Is The Countenance Of Pride.
~Offense Is The Enemy Of Agreement.
~Agreement Activates Faith.
~The Realm Of The Spirit Is Order.

~2~

OFFENSE: THE ORIGINAL SIN

Power Key: *Offense Was The Original Sin.*

heology supports the fall of man as the inception of sin. However, before there was sin in the garden, an insurrection erupted within the ranks of the angelic realm. The Book of Revelation Chapter 12 paints a descriptive picture of the event. *"And there was war in heaven: Michael and his angels fought against the dragon; and the dragon fought and his angels, and prevailed not..."* Long before the sad scene in the Garden of Eden, a revolt took place disrupting the flow of agreement among the Godhead.

Ezekiel 28 gives an account of the consequential fall of Lucifer. Although the Bible does not give full details, we can safely assume that Lucifer took offense with God. I believe, as Heaven's worship leader, Lucifer gradually grew increasingly jealous as God received the glory for the worship he provided. He was the model of perfection, full of wisdom and perfect in beauty. He was the anointed cherub ordained by God. He lived on the Holy Mount of God and was blameless in his ways from the day he was created.

Power Key: *Offense Is The Root Of All Sin.*

Because of his beauty and splendor, Lucifer became filled with pride, which led to his offense. Pride will always be uncovered when diagnosing the root of offense. The concept of worshipping God repulsed Lucifer creating envy within him. So Lucifer, soon to be renamed Satan, hatched a plan. He would seize control. He would organize a rebellion. He would become God. The unity, oneness and pristine agreement among the upper echelon of glory was disrupted through offense, thus Heaven became silent.

Unfortunately for Lucifer, God did not "agree to disagree" on the matter of agreement. Instead, with a flick of His little finger God hurled Satan, the chief worship leader, along with his choir, one-third of the heavenly host down to earth. What a tumble that was, all the way from the stunning environs of Heaven to lowly Earth far below! Jesus, an eyewitness to the scene, reported, *"I beheld Satan as lightning fall from heaven..."* *(Luke 10:18).*

Power Key: *Agreement Is Prerequisite To True Worship.*

Offense drives a wedge between a worshipper and God because it exalts self above God. Only the true worship of believers in agreement can now fill the chambers of Heaven.

Isaiah 14:12-15 (KJV), records the episode this way, *How art thou fallen from heaven, O Lucifer, son of the morning! How art thou cut down to the ground, which didst weaken the nations! For thou hast said in thine heart, I will ascend into heaven, I will exalt my throne above the stars of God: I will sit also upon the mount of the congregation, in the sides of the north: I will ascend above the heights of the clouds: I will be like the most high. Yet thou shalt be brought down to hell, to the sides of the pit.*

~The Original Sin~

This amazing episode is loaded with implications for believers. Ezekiel records that one-third of the Host of Heaven – *one-third!* – was cast out with Satan. It is chilling to consider that these angelic creatures resided in the splendors of Heaven and yet *chose to go their own way.*

The **original sin**, then, was not Adam and Eve's transgression in the garden, but Satan's offense in Heaven. Unfortunately, the original sin, like Satan, is alive and well on planet Earth. *Acts 24:16, Therefore I always exercise and discipline myself [mortifying my body, deadening my carnal affections, bodily appetites*

*and worldly desires, endeavoring in all respects] to have a clear (unshaken, blameless) conscience, **void of offense** toward God and toward men.* The Apostle Paul speaks of exercising self-control to keep from walking in offense with God and with men. It may sound simple, but it is often the small things that are difficult to overcome. This is not referring to some "big" carnal sin such as fornication. Christians tend to justify and lessen the consequential effects of internal, unseen matters, such as offense. Still, God's Word gives the directive to live peaceably with all men which means to live in agreement.

Romans 12:16a,18, Live in harmony with one another; do not be haughty (snobbish, high-minded, exclusive... If possible, as far as it depends on you, live at peace with everyone. Peace means *to **agree**, band together, commit, without any delay, to lighten the ship, "none of these things move me" and provide.* In other words, to live peaceably sometimes means to lighten the load. Remove excess baggage from your ship!

According to Strong's Concordance, the Greek word for offense, *skandalon,* originally meant a movable stick with bait used to catch animals. The word then came to denote a snare or stumbling block. Metaphorically, it signifies that which causes error or sin.

Whenever we stub our toes against something, our first instinct is usually to lash out at the offending object. We might kick, curse the object or if it is small enough, pick it up and hurl it away in contempt.

Jesus is referred to as the great "Stumbling Stone", the "Rock of Offense". Every one will eventually stumble up against Him. Although His great love woos us and draws us close, our innate sinfulness inevitably "stubs its toe" on His holiness.

Power Key: *The Clutter Of Our Disorder Creates A Barrier Between The Perfectness Of God And Us.*

The floodlights of His holiness illuminate our souls at the entrance of our relationship with the Lord Jesus. It is never a pretty picture. Like an X-ray riddled with blotches of cancer, we are all shot through and through with sin. Even on our best days, as the prophet Isaiah stated, *"We are no better than a pile of filthy rags."*

This concept is offensive even to the best of us. Be honest with yourself, most people think of themselves as being pretty decent. Although prone to some mischief, the occasional ugly thought, and a bad habit or two, they think to themselves, *"I'm not that bad."* Something in the fallen nature of man relentlessly tugs at the skirts of his soul and gives way to the death wish of offense. Even as ancient Israel stumbled on the rock of offense, Romans 9:32 says, " *...but Israel, pursuing the law of righteousness, has not attained to the law of righteousness. Why? Because they did not seek it by faith, but as it were, by the works of the law. For they stumbled at that stumbling stone."*

When believers stumble because of offense, much like Satan, they seek to drag others down. Just as misery loves company, so does offense. Consider the inappropriate incident in which Peter rebukes the Lord. Jesus was sharing with His disciples that He was about to suffer many things at the hands of the elders and the chief priests and scribes. Peter's rebuke stems from a self-centered motive. He says, *Matthew 16:22 (KJV), "Be it far from thee, Lord: this shall not be unto thee."* The well intended, but egocentric rebuke, made Peter an offense and an obstacle. Peter holds out a tantalizing enticement for Jesus to take offense: "After all, **You** are the Lord. Why should **You** suffer and be crucified? C'mon, let's get on with our mission to liberate Israel!"

~*Behaving Like Satan*~

The Lord refused the beguiling bait and avoided a scandalous predicament. He denied offense and remained true to His mission. His response to Peter, which may seem "brutal or insensitive" in our modern vernacular, speaks volumes today:

"Get thee behind me, Satan!"

Joe, one of the staff members of my church, is a talented mime. He and a partner often perform dramatic skits of the war between good and evil. Joe plays a very convincing Satan and "assails" his partner during their performances. Aided with make-up and dramatic music, the skits are riveting. Joe realized, one day, how realistic his performances were when he was riding an escalator in an area mall. Suddenly, he heard a child crying, "Mom! Mom! It's Satan! It's Satan!" Going up the escalator in the other direction was a frightened youngster who had attended one of their performances. Reflecting back, Joe now finds humor in the incident and remembers how chilling it was to be called Satan.

Imagine the Lord calling you Satan. Could there be a worse rebuke? Yet, there in black and white type, Jesus reprimands His number one disciple.

The Master poignantly delves into the heart of the issue with Peter, *"...for you are not setting your mind on God's interests, but man's."* Deep within, Peter sensed the truth of what Jesus was saying about the impending crucifixion. It offended him. The death of Jesus meant the derailment of Peter's dreams for earthly glory and power. Through the seductive power of offense, Peter sought to deter Jesus from His mission.

Jesus equates Peter with Satan, because his actions were so closely identifiable to Satan's mannerisms. Peter was acting like Satan. To become offended is to set your mind on your own interests. There is nothing more diabolical than selfishness. ***Just as humility is at the heart of agreement, pride is at the heart of offense.*** Becoming easily offended is proof of too much self. A thin-skinned individual is one dealing with pride. Slay the self, avoid becoming offended, then there will be nothing left to offend you. What a liberating discovery!

~Offended Worshippers~

As a worship leader, I love nothing more than accessing the presence of the Holy Spirit. You have very likely tasted the "beauty of holiness" and know the ecstasy of communing intimately with the Lord. The unmatchable, peerless, sweetness of the Holy Spirit's presence is available to all who walk in agreement. Why would anyone want to disrupt the precious flow of life, joy and power from the beloved Father?

Yet, often, I look up from my pulpit and catch glimpses of disgruntled persons here and there within the sanctuary, with arms crossed, angry countenances or bored expressions. From over a decade of experience as a pastor and worship leader, I have learned that a person's inability to enter into worship is usually because:

1) they have brought an offense into the worship service or

2) they have become offended at the prospect of submitting themselves to God in worship.

Either way, the offense wrecks their worship experience, stealing the joy, strength and renewal they could have received. It also robs everyone else in their world of the joy, strength and renewal, they could have imparted to them if they had entered into worship. It grieves me to see them miss out on worship, and angers me that they rob God of the worship He deserves – all due to offense.

Offended worshippers here on earth behave much like Lucifer did before his inglorious descent from his lofty position in Heaven. The worship flowed beautifully and still, Lucifer entertained offense and his spiraling downfall began.

~Offense Is A Choice~

Offense is a choice; just as agreement is a choice to submit oneself to another. To be disagreeable with another person is to embrace the spirit of Satan's original rebellion. I cannot emphasize this strongly enough. *There is nothing more diabolic and satanic than offense.*

Every time you start to become angry, remember there is nothing more evil than offense. If you harbor offense, it will eventually control you. With the stealth of a thief, offense will secretly take over your life.

Offense becomes a disposition, an attitude. If you are disagreeable with one boss, you will be disagreeable with another. If you disagree with one spouse and divorce him/her, you will do it again with another. Offense will follow you wherever you go.

This truly is a matter of life and death. Allowing offense to take root in your heart creates a possibility of severing your lifeline with God Himself. I recall, with a chill, hearing a woman say, "I'd rather go to hell than forgive so and so." Tragically, she meant it. Such is the place offense brings one to; thousands of people are disagreeing themselves right into hell.

~Checking For Offense~

What is upsetting you today? What is blocking your communion with the Holy Spirit? What is stealing your soul away from the precious presence of God? The Scriptures exhort, to sift your attitude and emotions.

Psalm 139:23-24, Search me O God and know my heart; test me and know my anxious thoughts. See if there be any offensive way in me, and lead me in the way everlasting.

Take a few minutes now to do an offense check. Write down the people's names against which you have some kind of grudge. These might include your spouse, children, relatives, boss, and business colleagues.

If you will honestly assess your life, you will be amazed at how disagreeable you really are.

"I did not like the pastor's message."
That is an offense.
"My parents do not understand me."
That is an offense.
"My father said such and such 20 years ago."
That is an offense.
"My husband was insensitive to me last night."
That is an offense.
"My boss is really piling on the work and he can be such a jerk."
That is an offense.
"My wife has not cleaned the house in two weeks."
That is an offense.

Disagreement is not simply a matter of arguing over a dinner menu, whether to serve baked or mashed potatoes. Disagreement is a matter of the heart. Thousands of Christians maintain a clean exterior image, attending church regularly, abstaining from alcohol, tobacco, and immorality. However, in the matters of the heart, millions of believers are missing the mark.

People harbor offense at their great peril. Offense destroys the Power of Agreement, severing the lifeline to the Holy Spirit.

Power Key: *Agreement Is The Absence Of Offense.*

The Body of Christ truly does not understand how

dangerous offense is. When you hold an offense against someone, even God is constrained and cannot help you. He will not violate His own principles, as confirmed in *Psalm 138:2, He will honor His word above all His name.*

In effect, offense communicates to God:
~"You made a mistake bringing this man or woman into my life."
~"You made a mistake bringing me to this church."
~"You made a mistake giving me this job, this family, this_____ (you fill in the blank)."

Many see no danger in retiring for the evening with angry and embittered hearts, even though Ephesians 4:26 clearly warns against it. Offense creates a separation between the believer and God, because God is Love. You cannot say you love someone when you remain offended with them. When you are offended, you are opposed to everything God stands for – ***everything***. *I Corinthians 13:4-7, Love endures long and is patient and kind; love never is envious nor boils over with jealousy, is not boastful or vainglorious, does not display itself haughtily. It is not conceited (arrogant and inflated with pride); it is not rude (unmannerly) and does not act unbecomingly. Love (God's love in us) does not insist on its own rights or its own way, for it is not self-seeking; it is not touchy or fretful or resentful; it takes no account of the evil done to it [it pays no attention to a suffered wrong]. It does not rejoice at injustice and unrighteousness, but rejoices when right and truth prevail. Love bears up under anything and everything that comes, is*

ever ready to believe the best of every person, its hopes are fadeless under all circumstances, and it endures everything [without weakening]. When you operate in offense and disagreement, you sever your lifeline to God's power. ***God is love – Love is agreement.***

The awful effect of offense in believers, multiplied millions of times, is creating havoc in the Church today. Precious spiritual power is siphoned away in small grudges, bitterness and pride. The cost is enormous, even delaying, I believe, the return of the Lord Jesus Christ.

Assessing the depths of disagreeableness is easy, like Paul in Romans 7 when he cried out, "Who will set me free from the body of this death?" Disagreement abounds in our world. But to play on Romans 5:20, *where disagreement abounds, agreement can abound all the more* – if we are willing to find the Agreeable Factor.

Ask God to pour His Anointing of Agreement upon your life right where you are. You must first remove all offense. *Agreement is the absence of offense.* Pray, in faith, agreeing for healing and forgiveness in this area.

PRAYER OF AGREEMENT:

Precious Holy Spirit, You are the Agreeable Factor of the Godhead. I pray, in the Name of the Father, the Son and the Holy Spirit; and come into agreement with Pastor Thomas Michael, as touching anything on earth, knowing that it shall be done of the Father Who is in Heaven. Holy Spirit forgive me of any and all offenses I am carrying or have carried in my heart. I want to be in

complete harmony with Your Character. You are gentle, meek, and lowly in heart; I take Your yoke upon me and find rest and quietness for my soul. I want to be like You. I choose Agreement over offense in the Name of the Father, the Son, Jesus Christ and the precious Holy Spirit, Who are Three – yet, One.

Amen

When you have prayed this prayer in faith, prepare to walk in the very anointing, the very essence that the Father, the Son and the Holy Spirit walk in. You will become more agreeable. You will take on...

...the **attitude** of Agreement which is submission.
...the **character** of Agreement which is humility.
...the **force** of Agreement which is obedience.
...the **product** of Agreement which is perseverance.
...the **fruit** of Agreement which is Favor.

Prepare yourself for the powerful currents of favor to begin flooding your life.

POWER KEYS:

~Offense Was The Original Sin.
~Offense Is The Root Of All Sin.
~Agreement Is Prerequisite To True Worship.
~The Clutter Of Our Disorder Creates A Barrier Between The Perfectness Of God And Us.
~Agreement Is The Absence Of Offense.

~*3*~

FINDING THE AGREEABLE FACTOR

Power Key: *Find The Agreeable Factor In Every Situation.*

ffense is inevitable. Jesus Himself said so in *Luke 17:1 (KJV), "It is impossible but that offense will come."* If offense is inevitable, how then does one deal with it?

In each situation of life lies the opportunity to agree with someone. Even in the most troubled circumstances, a gold nugget – an Agreeable Factor – glimmers. You simply must be willing to sift your soul to find it.

What exactly is the Agreeable Factor? It is flowing in a spirit of love, goodwill and generosity toward others at all times. It means refusing to allow your spirit to remain offended and disagreeable. It calls for finding the one thing in any given "disagreeable" circumstance in which you can agree with the "offending" person.

Let me give you an example from my own experience. For years, I showered my wife, Judy, with flowers, chocolates, and romantic cards. I thought the gifts made her feel loved. However, over time I have discovered what she really craves from me is tenderness, understanding and, that most precious of all commodities for a busy pastor, my time. Sometimes, when she explained to me that the gifts, while nice, were not what she really desired, I became offended. I expressed my love for her in a way that made me feel good. To find the Agreeable Factor, however, I have learned to agree with Judy on what makes her feel loved. *Psalm 119:165 (KJV), Great peace have they that love thy law, and nothing shall offend them.*

~Finding The Agreeable Factor~

Finding the Agreeable Factor is often a bloody business. Worldly wisdom, such as my mistaken notions of romance, must die. To become agreeable one must become a servant, always sensitive to what is best for others. Bit by bit learn to slay the self.

The Agreeable Factor extends to entities as well as to people. A friend of mine recently had to ante up some taxes to good old Uncle Sam. He felt disagreeable about it and found himself grumbling about government waste. He was offended at the prospect of sending money to an organization often inefficient and wasteful.

Then he sensed the nudge of the Holy Spirit gently

warning him that he was about to develop an attitude of offense. So he spoke a brief prayer of blessing over our government and national leaders, thanked God for the many good things they provide and for the good roads, clean water and freedom we all enjoy in America. Suddenly, he was humming "God Bless America", swelling with patriotism! He had found the Agreeable Factor! In the span of two minutes, like an obedient soldier, his attitude did a quick about-face. The result was feelings of peace and goodwill toward the government and a willing release of his money. *Proverbs 18:19, A brother offended is harder to be won over than a strong city, and [their] contentions separate them like the bars of a castle.*

To disagree with someone, even a huge entity like the government, is to want things your own way. Remember the famous fast food jingle? "Have it your way! Have it your way!" The concept behind the ad was that everyone could have their hamburger made exactly as they desired. What if this concept was adapted and attitudes were adjusted to reflect, "Have it *your* way"?

This is the spirit of the Agreeable Factor, letting others have their way. It may sound simple, but all can attest when emotions of anger and offense arise, it is extremely difficult to find anything agreeable about the offending person.

The first step in finding the Agreeable Factor in any given situation is to confess your disagreement to the Lord. If you are in offense, it is safe to assume you are in sin. It is important to restore your agreement with God before you can agree with the offending person. Ask God for strength to find agreement. As the Lord said in *John 15:5, "...apart from Me you can do nothing."* Thank God for the opportunity to grow in agreement.

Power Key: *Agreement Is The Catalyst For Growth.*

Take the initiative to find the Agreeable Factor. For example, if I disagree with my wife over a matter, my position should not be to persuade her to have the same idea. The opposing person should find the Agreeable Factor. You must take the initiative and agree with your opponent. As Jesus said in *Matthew 5:25 (KJV), "Agree with thine adversary quickly, whiles thou art in the way with him..."* It is astounding how quickly the other party becomes peaceful and amicable.

You may be thinking that there are abusive and grossly immoral circumstances in which it is impossible to find the Agreeable Factor. For example, should a woman agree with being beaten by her abusive husband? If someone disputes the divinity of Jesus, saying He was a good man, but not the Son of God, should we agree? Of course not. *Finding the Agreeable Factor does not mean compromising your convictions and morals.*

~David And The Offended King~

Consider how David handled the evil treachery of King Saul. Proud, deluded and murderous, Saul stalked David for years in the desert. How does one find the Agreeable Factor with such a man? Through the power of the Holy Spirit, David did. He refused offense, honoring Saul's position as God's anointed king. He refused to strike Saul down when he had the opportunity to do so. Agreement did not mean putting himself in harm's way of a tormented, self-destructive leader. For David it meant honoring Saul's position as king and refusing to take matters into his own hands.

When you encounter situations where you know you are right, you may have more information than the other person or insight from the Holy Spirit. Under these circumstances, how can you possibly agree with the other person? It is not an issue about being right or wrong. It is about living peaceably with those around you.

~*It Is Okay To Be Wrong*~

Dare to be wrong. This may sound crazy, but it is gloriously freeing to admit you are wrong even when you are right. The truly humble person does not care whether they are right or wrong. They have no ravenous "self" to feed or aspirations for small victories of self-justification. Always remember, any attempt to justify yourself ushers you into satanic territory. When you know you are right in a particular circumstance, and you try to prove you are right, you end up being in the wrong because of pride and offense.

Consider the supreme example of Jesus as Pilate interrogated Him; Jesus spoke not a word in an attempt to justify himself. "Don't you know I have the power to free you?" Pilate asked, astonished that Jesus would "squander" His life. With supernatural self-restraint, Jesus remained silent. With the same anointing and essence of agreement in the Godhead, Jesus found the Agreeable Factor. No, He did not agree with Pilate's injustice and the ensuing torture. However, He did agree with the Father's plan for the redemption of mankind. He submitted Himself to a torturous death whose cost was incredibly high, because of His agreement with His purpose.

Power Key: *Agreement Unlocks The Favor Of God.*

Jesus agreed with God about completing the terrible work of the cross "for the joy" set before Him. Agreement is costly, but the reward of joy more than makes up for the loss. Agreement unlocks the favor of God!

One woman I knew worked in an intense sales environment where everyone pointed fingers of blame whenever something went wrong in the office. No one would accept responsibility for problems and mistakes. For a few months, this lady joined in the game. She was soon exhausted and frustrated, trying to place blame where it belonged. Finally, she began to accept responsibility for problems that occurred in the office. Rather than burning up valuable time and energy on arguments and finger pointing, she began to say, "You know, I agree that's my fault. I will own this problem. I'll take care of it."

The winsome, joyful way she accepted responsibility astonished her colleagues. Gradually, her agreeable spirit began convicting her co-workers of their wrong attitudes and they began accepting responsibility for mistakes and problems. The atmosphere in the office began to change for the better.

When you pay the price to find the Agreeable Factor, you are in essence making an exchange with God, His character in exchange for your poor attitude.

Power Key: *The Fruit Of Agreement Is Favor.*

Consider the children of Israel as they stood on the brink of the Promised Land, a land fertile beyond their wildest dreams, a land "flowing with milk and honey". Moses sent 12 spies to scout out the land and bring back a report. They were sent to find the Agreeable Factor – confirmation of God's promise of a place of abundance. Moreover, they found it and returned with a gargantuan cluster of grapes. The Bible tells us that the 12 spies went in agreement and confirmed that it was a land flowing with milk and honey. The cluster of grapes was the fruit produced through agreement!

Moses had told them the land would be flowing with milk and honey (good things) and so it was. Then, in one of those horrible moments of history, the jaws of defeat snipped the wings of victory and the spies lunged into negativity, resulting in disagreement.

A very interesting thing happens at this point. Moses' right hand man, Joshua, was in agreement with him. Joshua also needed someone to agree with him and God sent Caleb. God will always provide someone with whom to agree.

Power Key: *When Agreement Is Present, Offense Is Always Lurking.*

Opposition is often evidence that you are in right agreement with someone. When you enter into agreement with someone, it often means disconnecting with others. Not all agreement yields good fruit and increase. It is easy to align yourself with people who are detrimental to your spiritual well being. Negative, disagreeable people are always at hand. It would have been far easier for Caleb and Joshua to go with the crowd. Instead, they courageously remained in their agreement with God's promise. ***Agreement produces passion.*** Joshua and Caleb's agreement is evident, in Numbers 14:6, as they tear their clothes in anguish at the growing rebellion of the people. Caleb tries mightily to recoup the agreement, but fails:

Numbers 13:30-33 (KJV), And Caleb stilled the people before Moses, and said, Let us go up at once, and possess it; for we are well able to overcome it. But the men that went up with him said, We be not able to go up against the people; for they are stronger than we. And they brought up an evil report of the land which they had searched unto the children of Israel, saying, The land, through which we have gone to search it, is a land that eateth up the inhabitants thereof; and all the people that we saw in it are men of a great stature... and we were in our own sight as grasshoppers, and so we were in their sight.

Then Joshua joined Caleb in pleading with the people while a blaze of disagreement and offense – lit by the 10 offended spies – roared through the entire camp.

Numbers 14:8-9 (KJV), If the Lord delight in us, then he will bring us into this land, and give it us, a land which floweth with milk and honey. Only rebel not ye against the Lord, neither fear ye the people of the land; for they are bread for us: their defense is departed from them, and the Lord is with us: fear them not.

Only do not rebel! To be offended is to rebel and breach the agreement. Too many Christians put their "but" into everything. Rather than walking in obedience, they say, "But Pastor," "But God, it's so hard," "But God, I feel afraid," But God . . ."

In Numbers 14, the "entire congregation" murmured and complained, thus nullifying – the agreement with God. *(KJV), Would God that we had died in the land of Egypt! or would God we had died in this wilderness!* Little did they know, God would grant them their wish. All of them would perish in the wilderness during the next 40 years. Joshua and Caleb remained faithful to their agreement and got their wish: two all-expense-paid passes into the glorious Promised Land. Joshua and Caleb held onto the Agreeable Factor, and only they eventually reaped the reward.

Power Key: ***The Fulfillment Of The Agreement Is The Promise.***

"We seemed like grasshoppers," cried the Israelites, because their focus was on the problem and not the promise. The Canaanites, who possessed the land, were no threat to the Israelites. God had been with them

throughout their journey in the desert sustaining them, yet, they chose to fix their minds on the disagreeable factor. The Promised Land had been pledged to them by God; surely, He could handle a few giants. Only those who embraced the agreeable factor inherited the Promised Land and the rest died in the wilderness!

Power Key: *Attention To The Disagreeable Factor Is The Disarmament Of Promised Victory.*

Can you sense the propensity I feel about this agreeable factor? It truly can become a matter of life and death. It is quite apparent the same kind of problems exist today, as with the ten unbelieving spies. Disbelief caused by disagreement is the cause of much of the lack present among God's people today as in the days of Moses. If you repeatedly fail to believe the Word of God, which is the *good report*, you will easily believe the *bad report*. The Bible is clear regarding the outcome of believing the bad report – you will faint. *"Be not weary in well doing, for in due season you shall reap if you faint not."* If you continually faint at the smallest of obstacles, you will, like the Israelites, declare yourself a grasshopper amidst the face of society's low standards.

"Whose report will you believe?" question the Scriptures. Indeed, whose report will you believe?

I want to encourage you to decide today to find the Agreeable Factor in every situation. Instead of complaining, begin to agree. It does not mean you compromise your standards; rather, it causes you to flow in the fruit of the Spirit.

The choice is yours. The line Moses drew in the sand

for the children of Israel, so many centuries ago, as recorded in *Deuteronomy 30:19*, is still there today: *"I set before you today life and death . . . so choose life."*

Choose life! Choose agreement! You will never be the same!

PRAYER OF AGREEMENT:

Dear Lord, Thank You for helping me find the Agreeable Factor in every situation. I choose to walk in agreement with those whom You have placed in my life. Forgive me for those times when I have focused on the negative instead of the agreeable. In the Name of the Father, the Son and the Holy Ghost.

Amen

POWER KEYS:

~Find The Agreeable Factor In Every Situation.
~Agreement Is The Catalyst For Growth.
~Agreement Unlocks The Favor Of God.
~The Fruit Of Agreement Is Favor.
~When Agreement Is Present, Offense Is Always Lurking.
~The Fulfillment Of The Agreement Is The Promise.
~Attention To The Disagreeable Factor Is The Disarmament Of Promised Victory.

~4~

AGREEMENT WITH AUTHORITY

Power Key: *Agreement With Authority Creates Success.*

eace accompanies honor when it is bestowed upon authority. *I Thessalonians 5: 12,13, Now also we beseech you, brethren, get to know those who labor among you [recognize them for what they are, acknowledge and appreciate and respect them all]- your leaders who are over you in the Lord and those who warn and kindly reprove and exhort you. And hold them in very high and most affectionate esteem in [intelligent and sympathetic] appreciation of their work. Be at peace among yourselves.* The apostle was referring to a peace that was absent of offense. It is impossible to properly honor those in authority over you without living peaceably with others.

In his fine book, *God's Armor-Bearer*, Terry Nance describes the challenges and rewards of serving as an associate pastor for many years. One of Nance's comments especially struck me. He says, "God made us all different. At least 50% of the time, your pastor's way of doing things will differ from yours." *Half of the time!* One would think that agreement with the man of God would flow naturally. Nance explains, if your goal is to further the kingdom, the method used to achieve this end does not become the focus, instead, the end result. After all, this person was selected by God to instruct in spiritual matters, to rebuke, to exhort and to encourage. ***Agreement looks at the office of the man in authority, not at his individuality***. Although a pastor spends significant time in Bible study and prayer, it does not automatically mean one should agree with his decisions 100% of the time.

Power Key: *The Virtuous Acts Of A Man Of God Are Imitable.*

As a pastor and human being, let me be the first to declare that men of God are not perfect! I have intimate, first-hand knowledge of this phenomenon (and so does my wife)! Yet, I have found that when my congregation will "go with the flow" of the Holy Spirit and obey the instructions I receive from God, no matter how preposterous they may seem, the result is always positive. The writer of Hebrews exhorts the reader to remember those in authority because they are the messengers of the Word. *Hebrews 13:7,17, Remember your leaders and superiors*

in authority [for it was they] who brought to you the Word of God. Observe attentively and consider their manner of living (the outcome of their wellspent lives) and imitate their faith (their conviction that God exists and is the Creator and Ruler of all things, the Provider and Bestower of eternal salvation through Christ, and their leaning of the entire human personality on God in absolute trust and confidence in His power, wisdom, and goodness). Obey your spiritual leaders and submit to them [continually recognizing their authority over you], for they are constantly keeping watch over your souls and guarding your spiritual welfare, as men who will have to render an account [of their trust]. [Do your part to] let them do this with gladness and not with sighing and groaning, for that would not be profitable to you [either]. **When a church agrees with the authority of the house, everyone reaps the reward of obedience – the favor of God!**

The key is agreement, not perfection. Nance raises a point that is pivotal for our spiritual well-being. He regularly chose to agree with his pastor's decisions and directions even when he disagreed. His agreeable nature made all the difference in the fulfillment of his own dreams and goals. Remember my definition of agreement from Chapter One about laying down your dreams? *I Peter 5:5, Likewise, you who are younger and of lesser rank, be subject to the elders (the ministers and spiritual guides of the church) – [giving them due respect and yielding to their counsel]. Clothe (apron) yourselves, all of you, with humility [as the garb of a servant, so that its covering cannot possibly be stripped from you, with free-*

dom from pride and arrogance] toward one another. For God sets Himself against the proud (the insolent, the overbearing, the disdainful, the presumptuous, the boastful) – [and He opposes, frustrates and defeats them], but gives grace (favor, blessing) to the humble. Your willingness to humble yourself, as unto the Lord to those in authority over you, will produce the fruit of agreement – Favor.

Power Key: *The Act Of Agreement Is Laying Down One's Dreams And Embracing The Dreams Of Another.*

The Bible instructs on the importance and blessedness of obeying the man of God, even when his instruction seems undesirable, unreasonable or does not make sense. One of the most difficult tasks believers will ever have is agreeing with the spiritual head God places over their lives. Since the Garden of Eden, mankind has shirked authority like a filthy child fleeing a steaming bathtub brimming with soapy bubbles. Often, the man of God is met with the same response, an obstinate and rebellious attitude. You will never find your purpose until you learn how to submit to the man of God in your life.

For centuries, God has equipped the Church with teachers, prophets, pastors and apostles to lead in the ways of God. He has given these men and women special insight, direction and instruction. When honor is bestowed upon the man of God, you are ultimately honoring and obeying God. I like the way my dear friend, Dr. Murdock puts it: "Your reaction to a man of God will determine God's reaction to you."

There are countless blessings that have been delayed, if not aborted completely, because of harboring offense with the man of God. For years, I have heard people who have attended my church say, "I enjoy your church, but I don't agree with everything you say."

When does anyone ever agree on everything? No one ever will. Every human is a complicated universe unto themselves with a unique history and set of experiences. In any group of two or more, there will never be complete agreement on everything.

Intellectual and/or emotional agreement is not the point. Agreement is not a wave of "goose bump emotions" or a perfect alignment of theologies. Emotions can interfere and even eradicate the power of agreement. The anointing of agreement is the same spirit that the Father, the Son and the Holy Spirit operate in – they continually and unceasingly flow in unity.

Power Key: *Agreement With The Man Of God Is Always An Available Source To Discover God's Will.*

Agreement is a choice to set aside your own will and embrace God's will instead. Whether your emotions or intellect like it, agreement with a man of God is the most valuable channel God has for communicating with His people. *Amos 3:7, Surely the Lord God will do nothing without revealing His secret to His servants the prophets.* What better way does God have to reveal His plan in your life than through the one who watches over your soul?

Tens of thousands of believers routinely shuttle from church to church, from meeting to meeting, seeking a man of God who agrees with them. Notice I said "agrees with them". They really do not seek someone to agree with; instead, like a god unto themselves (Remember Satan's attitude in the first fall?), they want the man of God to agree with their ideas. They settle into a particular church for a few weeks or months, praising the Lord and rejoicing. When the pastor says or does something they do not approve of, like a piece of unchewed meat, it does not quite settle in their craw. Perhaps, their man of God gives them an instruction that makes them feel uncomfortable, forcing them to make changes to their lifestyle and nudging them into humility.

~Agreement Is Not An Option!~

It is impossible to enter into relationship with a man of God when your heart is filled with bitterness, unforgiveness, offense and pride. There is no hope for an impartation of the wisdom of God with offense present. Your pastor can only present the Word; it is up to you to have an agreeable, open heart free from offense to receive it.

Agreement is not an option! When you serve the God of Agreement, you must agree! In the Old Testament, God placed as much focus on the consequence of sin and rebellion as he did the reward of obedience. He gave much thought to the consequence of breaking covenant. This is not only an issue for the agreement breakers of the Old Testament, but for those in the New Testament as well. *Romans 1:28-32 (KJV), And even as they did not like to retain God in their knowledge, God gave them over to a reprobate mind, to do those things which are not convenient; being filled with all unrighteousness, fornication, wickedness, covetousness, maliciousness; full of envy, murder, debate, deceit, malignity, whispers, backbiters, haters of God, despiteful, proud, boasters, inventors of evil things, disobedient to parents, without understanding, **covenantbreakers**, without natural affection, implacable, unmerciful: who knowing the judgment of God, that they which commit such things are worthy of death, not only do the same, but have pleasure in them that do them.*

That is quite a line up of shady characters. In the midst of all those reprobates, you find the agreement breakers. The punishment is rather severe. You may say, "Just because they broke a little agreement?" "What's the wrong in coming out of agreement with one pastor as long as you move into agreement with another?" Herein lies the danger, most Christians who have gone AWOL (absent with out leave) seldom move into agreement with another man of God. They remain in a lawless condition. An individual who is *absent-without-leave* from the Armed Forces of our country is considered a criminal. People who come out of agreement with whom God has assigned them to, "church-hop" until they find another truce-breaker. ***The moment you step out of agreement with a divine connection in your life, you enter into covenant with an impaired army of impotent people.*** They wander from church to church and from relationship to relationship trying to find something that is only found in the original covenant.

It is quite obvious we are living in the dispensation of the age of grace and God is not going to kill someone who breaks an agreement with a divine connection. However, covenant breakers usually wander around with no purpose, no direction, and no connection. In essence, they are like "dead people walking".

People who breach an agreement could possibly be part of the great company of those who will fall away. *II Thessalonians 2:3 (KJV), Let no man deceive you by any means: for that day shall not come, except there come a falling away first and that man of sin be revealed, the son of* **perdition** *–* **death**...

If you are connected to the vine you will have no fear of ever falling away. It is only those who have no authority to agree with that are not connected. Everyone must agree with someone.

~A Surge Of Favor~

Agreement is like a current of electricity. When you connect to a power source you become illuminated. Connected Christians are lit up! They shine like beacons and search lights in a dark world. The pastor assigned to you by God carries the right voltage for your connection. When a believer decides within himself who should be his spiritual leader, it is like plugging your blow dryer into the clothes dryer outlet. Too many immature Christians try to connect their 120 volt plug into a pastor with 220 volts. That is when circuits get blown and the power goes out!

Perhaps, God has connected you with a 220 volt

pastor and you are a 120; this requires a converter. The converter transforms the energy from 220 to 120. It absorbs the extra power and makes it receptive to the lower voltage. Your converter is the Holy Spirit. He converts what your pastor teaches and turns it into something you can receive. You must humble yourself and stay connected to your pastor, regardless of what he throws at you. You may be feeling like your pastor is overloading you. Not to worry, the Holy Spirit is also your surge protector.

Are you plugged into the right outlet, or has your power been terminated? Get plugged in and stay connected. Get ready for the currents of favor to surge through your life.

~Lawlessness~

In this same chapter, the Bible speaks of the spirit of lawlessness. *II Thessalonians 2:4,7, Who opposes and exalts himself so proudly and insolently against and over all that is called God or that is worshiped, [even to his actually] taking his seat in the temple of God, proclaiming that he himself is God. For the mystery of lawlessness (that hidden principle of rebellion against constituted authority) is already at work in the world, [but it is] restrained only until he who restrains is taken out of the way.*

This spirit is a result of the mystery of lawlessness which is the spirit of offense. Lucifer embodied the same spirit when he was cast out from his worship leader's position in Heaven. The same spirit moved through

Judas when he became offended. *John 12:3 (KJV), Then took Mary a pound of ointment of spikenard, very costly, and anointed the feet of Jesus, and wiped his feet with her hair; and the house was filled with the odour of the ointment. Then saith one of his disciples, Judas Iscariot, Simon's son, which should betray him, why was not this ointment sold for three hundred pence, and given to the poor? This he said, not that he cared for the poor; but because he was a thief, and had the bag, and bare what was put therein.* Judas was offended at the prospect that Mary was pouring out an expensive bottle of perfume that could have been sold for a large sum of money.

The punishment God often rendered to Israel was always with the intent to bring them back into (covenant) agreement. God's wrath was often kindled against His children because He simply could not stand to watch His own going without. Jehovah-Jireh, "Our Provider", hates lack! God wants you to be blessed and to live more abundantly. He wants you to walk in divine favor.

In the Book of Leviticus Chapter 26, God lays out His vengeful plans against His children for breaking the covenant agreement. He carefully details what He is going to do to them. Then in verses 44 and 45 He says, "*And yet for all that, when they be in the land of their enemies, I will not cast them away, neither will I abhor them, to destroy them utterly, and to break my covenant with them: for I Am the Lord their God.*"

~Conditions For Agreement~

The Israelites' attitudes were disquieting to God

and yet, He was subdued and brought His wrath under control simply because of His agreement with them. Before you become too relaxed, thinking it is all right to break agreements, think again. God does not have a problem forgiving you. However, He will allow you to move into the middle of a treacherous situation when you become surrounded by your enemies and then, He will rescue you.

You must understand that God cannot and will not fulfill His covenants with men while they are in rebellion. Rewards are reserved for the obedient. There must be repentance and submission to the terms of the agreement before there can be any fulfillment of promise. The theory of unconditional agreement is idle fantasy. In order to enjoy the benefits of an agreement you must meet the conditions.

When God wants to bless you, He places a right person in your life.

Consider the widow of Zarephath in the Book of I Kings. The prophet Elijah asked her to give him the last of her flour – an audacious request considering her starving circumstances. The fact that she was a widow tells us, perhaps, she had already lost her husband to the famine, increasing her reluctance to share any of the rations left to her and her son.

Viewed in a negative light, as we are wont to do, Elijah's request appears selfish. Nevertheless, the widow obeyed; and as a result, she, her son and the man of God ate for an entire year in the middle of famine! *That is the Favor of God!*

The moment you come into agreement with the

man of God, what you desire is done in Heaven by the Father.

You must learn to come into agreement with the man of God in your life, then your tithes will rebuke the devourer and your prayers will go unhindered. When you resent and reject a man of God you automatically breach your agreement with him. Everyone desperately needs the covering and protection of a spiritual shepherd. The enemy picks off wandering sheep.

Power Key: *Agreement Provides Protection.*

It is not out of order to disagree, at times, with how your pastor runs his church or what he preaches. As I mentioned earlier, no one will ever agree on everything. What is not acceptable is taking offense against a man of God. Do not let offense take root in your heart. It is not enough to simply pray the prayer of agreement with someone, then turn around and criticize him or her in disagreement. The seeds that you sow into a ministry are seeds sown in agreement with the one receiving the offering. The moment you become offended with the recipient of the seed, you have come out of the agreement.

Sometimes the seed you sow is transported on your pastor's faith. The Bible tells us to give according to what one has purposed in the heart. You may not have enough faith to even reach out for an envelope. God provides one with whom you can agree.

Power Key: *As Long As There Is Someone To Agree With, There Is Always Hope For A Brighter Day.*

Liking the man of God is not a prerequisite for agreement. You must find the agreeable factor. You can always agree in Jesus' Name.

I have purposed to stay in agreement with the members of my church who have sown into my life. I liken myself unto a scarecrow that keeps away the thieving birds that could devour their crop.

Authority works within the law of agreement. Your man of God plays a key role in your life. You cannot function alone. God uses different sources to speak to His children. Can you hear God speaking? You may think your pastor is too hard on you, or that the word he delivers is not sweet. God speaks through your shepherd and his voice will be the gentlest voice God uses. Do not murmur against authority.

~Offense With The Man Of God~

The moment you become offended with a man of God, whether he is your pastor, a visiting evangelist, or the author of the book you are reading, you must stop everything you are doing and repent. Remember, your man of God is doing the best he can. Like you, he has blind spots and weaknesses. According to Scripture, your reaction to his imperfections may very well be your shortcomings as well. *Romans 2:1-3, Therefore you have no excuse or defense or justification, O man, whoever you are who judges and condemns another. For imposing as judge and passing sentence on another, you condemn yourself, because you who judge are habitually practicing the very same things [that you censor and*

denounce]. [But] we know that the judgment (adverse verdict, sentence) of God falls justly and in accordance with truth upon those who practice such things. And do you think or imagine, O man, when you judge and condemn those who practice such things and yet do them yourself, that you will escape God's judgment and elude His sentence and adverse verdict?

Power Key: *Never Take Offense With One Who Can Deliver You.*

If you have been unsuccessful in finding the agreeable factor with a man of God, because of rebellion on your part, you may choose to leave. You have taken matters into your own hands. Or you may be in the wrong church. As my precious friend Dr. Zonnya puts it: "This is my ballpark! You choose to play by the owner's (your pastor's) rules and stay with joy. Play by your own rules and remain with conflict or get out!"

Your lack of agreement with a man of God may be a red flag that you are with the wrong congregation. From my experience, however, most people usually exit a church because they have chosen offense and disagreement over God's geographical assignment for their lives.

If you struggle in agreeing with the spiritual head God has placed over your life, I urge you to relax and "go with the flow." Guard what you say. Never cut down the man or woman of God. Do not let his or her faults discourage you. Stay out of his personal life – it is none of your business. Too many churches place their pastors under a microscope dissecting their every move. They eventually suffocate the gift within the man and sever their own life source. Instead, churches should refrain from judging and criticizing and allow the Lord to administer His correction. If he goes astray, God will bring him back into the right path.

At all costs, agree with the man of God.

PRAYER OF AGREEMENT:

Heavenly Father, I ask You to forgive me for any rebellion on my part with the men and women of God in my life. Lord, please help me to walk humbly with those in authority over me. I will stay in agreement with my pastor and those whom You have placed over me. In the Name of the Father, the Son and the Holy Ghost.

Amen

POWER KEYS:

~Agreement With Authority Creates Success.
~The Virtuous Acts Of A Man Of God Are Imitable.
~The Act Of Agreement Is Laying Down One's Dreams And Embracing The Dreams Of Another.
~Agreement With The Man Of God Is Always An Available Source To Discover God's Will.
~Agreement Provides Protection.
~As Long As There Is Someone To Agree With, There Is Always Hope For A Brighter Day.
~Never Take Offense With One Who Can Deliver You.

~5~

AGREEMENT WITH YOUR PURPOSE

Power Key: *Agreement Is The Master Key To Anything Desired From God.*

ost everyone knows someone who carries a key that opens all the doors in a particular building. It is like magic, as the owner of the key proceeds down a hallway, one lock after another yielding to the *Master Key*. *Agreement is the Master Key* to anything desired from God. The person who allows agreement to flow through their spirit will suddenly find the doors to joy, prosperity, peace, health, and happiness opening.

Power Key: *Agreement Is The Foundation For Perpetual Prosperity.*

Luke 1:46-50 (KJV), And Mary said, My soul doth magnify the Lord, And my spirit hath rejoiced in God my Saviour. For he hath regarded the low estate of his handmaiden: for, behold, from henceforth all generations shall call me blessed. For he that is mighty hath done to me great things; and holy is his name. And his mercy is on them that fear him from generation to generation.

~*Mary's Agreement*~

Mary, the mother of Jesus, found the Master Key to her purpose. Before the doors to the blessings of God could open, she had to agree with her assignment from God. May I pose before you a "what-if"? What if Mary's child had been destined to be just another baby until she agreed with the messenger of God? What if Mary had not been the first human God attempted to use to carry out His plan of salvation? What if there were other young women who received this distinguished invitation, but refused to agree with the plan? Perhaps, there were others far more suitable for the assignment. However, their fear of the possibilities of persecution, even death, for the implication of "premarital sex" dissuaded them. Whatever the scenario, one thing is certain, Mary was favored of God. Remember, *the fruit of agreement is favor.* She was selected not because of her looks, because God is not into flesh. She was favored because of her agreeable, obedient spirit. Her assignment called for thirty years of people's false accusations, judgments, and gossip. There was probably not a day she went without having to overhear the whispers of the religious. ***In the***

midst of righteous persecution, there is always great favor with God. You must purpose in your heart to keep the agreeable factor ever before you. The book of Jeremiah states, *"Be not afraid of them [their faces], for I am with you to deliver you, says the Lord."*

Mary moved from a brief moment of doubt, "How can this be, I have never even known a man?", into a full-blown leap of faith and she agreed! She exploded into a rhapsody of joy in anticipation of what was to be.

*Luke 1:28-30, And he came to her and said, Hail, O favored one [endued with grace]! The Lord is with you! Blessed (**favored of God**) are you before all other women! But when she saw him, she was greatly troubled and disturbed and confused at what he said and kept revolving in her mind what such a greeting might mean. And the angel said to her, Do not be afraid, Mary, for you have found grace (**free, spontaneous, absolute favor** and lovingkindness) with God!*

This startling scene in Nazareth was a divine *"suddenly"* when God made an unexpected visitation into the life of mankind. God is a God of surprises. He delights in suddenly pulling back the veil separating the supernatural from the natural and revealing a glimpse of Himself.

Operating in the favor of God means moving into a relationship with Him that causes Him to bless you freely and spontaneously. It is receiving the abundant blessings of God without asking. Have you ever been blessed unexpectedly by someone you love? Whether with a simple gesture of kindness or the thoughtfulness of a greeting card or by the surprise of an elaborate gift. The result is still the same; you feel special. Like the stunned

Mary, one can only stammer in amazement. Nothing is impossible through the power of agreement!

The Book of Luke states, *"For with God nothing is ever impossible and no word from God shall be without power or impossible of fulfillment."* It was **the** crucial moment of Mary's life. The Lord, through the angel Gabriel, was asking Mary to agree with her purpose in life – to bear the Son of God. It was the zinger of zingers. It was not an out-of-left-field message – it was an out-of-outer-space surprise!

Perhaps, you have had similar experiences. After years in the business world, you may have rediscovered a talent that has lain dormant. Maybe, the Holy Spirit is nudging you to go on a mission trip this summer – and the sign-up deadline has arrived. Suddenly, you must make a decision.

Mary had no time to "think about it", to "pray about it" or "talk it over" with her girlfriends. Note that God was not *asking* for her permission. The whole plan is stated as fact, as a done deal; it was the *will* of God.

- You **will** conceive in your womb, and bear a son...
- And you **shall** name Him Jesus...
- He **will** be great...
- And **will** be called the Son of the Most High...
- And the Lord God **will** give Him the throne of His father David...
- And He **will** reign over the house of Jacob forever...
- And His kingdom **will** have no end...
- The Holy Spirit **will** come upon you...
- And the power of the Most High **will** overshadow you...

- And for that reason the Holy Offspring **will** be called the Son of God.

Can you see what God was trying to convey to Mary about what was transpiring in her life at that very moment? Did you detect the repetitive usage of the word "will"? When God speaks His *will*, it *will* be done. You can always count on it!

Power Key: *Satan Cannot Violate The Boundaries Of God's Will For Your Life.*

There were not enough demons in hell to stop the powerful plan God had written out in Mary's agreement for her life. When a person draws up a will under our governing laws, no one but the testator may make any adjustments or changes.

Satan can never breach the agreement between your life and God's will as long as you remain in agreement. Agreement provides boundaries that Satan cannot cross.

I become rather frustrated when I hear ministers on television and in pulpits glorifying Satan's power and ability to work in Christian's lives. The Child that Mary was carrying was the only other Being, besides the Holy Spirit, with any kind of power for being omnipresent and omniscient. Satan cannot be at all places at all times nor does he have the ability to know everything you think.

⚜

~Angels Outnumber Demons~

I believe that Satan's focus is mainly upon people who have the power to influence many. There are demons that lurk about each child of God, but remember, Satan took only one-third of the heavenly host. This tells us that for every demon on earth there are two angels in Heaven ready to thwart their plans against us. Praise the Lord! That is an awesome revelation. If one-third of the angels became demons, then two-thirds remained in the original agreement with God and are available for combat. I am not talking about angels who are novices in their jobs. These angels have been walking in agreement with God for millions of years; they know their assignments. Satan's demons have only been in operation since the revolt in Heaven.

Never underestimate the power of agreement. It is the foundation of the success of Heaven. In Luke 9:1, Jesus called together the Twelve and gave them power and authority over all demons. They did not have this power until He gave it to them. ***On your weakest day, you have more power than the devil; the only requirement is walking in agreement.***

How would you like to wake up every morning knowing that you had already defeated every demonic foe? Choose to walk in agreement. Choose to be free from offense. The entry of offense is the gateway to demonic oppression.

You can always count on God's will, but can He count on you to agreeably participate? Mary's purpose hung in the balance during those eternal seconds while

Gabriel awaited her response. Was all of Heaven leaning forward on tiptoes breathlessly awaiting the response of the fragile, human receptacle of God's grace? It was a moment of wonder and awe.

Power Key: *The Opportunity For Agreement Is Often, But For A Moment.*

Mary struggled momentarily, but mightily. The Amplified Bible describes the scene: *Luke 1:29, But when she saw him, she was greatly **troubled** and **disturbed** and **confused** at what he said and kept revolving in her mind what such a greeting might mean.*

Can you relate? Sometimes, the situations in life are so complex, so unsolvable, and a bit bizarre. We tend to think that if we simply revolve a problem around in our minds, like gerbils running on a treadmill, we will figure it out.

I think God was confident of Mary's decision. He knew her to be a humble, *agreeable* person. He knew He could count on her. Nevertheless, there was still this little matter of the *will* to resolve – the little matter of *agreement.* Would Mary lay down her dreams of a nice, normal life in the suburbs of Nazareth and pleasant years with her husband, Joseph, and a couple of kids with a mini-van in the driveway? Would she lay down those dreams and embrace God's dream? Would she be the vessel through whom God birthed His Son to become a ransom for mankind and her as well?

After laying out God's magnificent – albeit mind-boggling – plan, Gabriel plays a final card in verse 37 of the same chapter, *"For nothing will be impossible with God."*

It is almost as though Mary needed that last nudge. This statement must have charged Mary's faith and she quickly agreed.

Power Key: *The Marriage Of Faith And Agreement Produces The Impossible.*

She felt assurance that, although the situation was humanly impossible, it was a piece of cake for Almighty God.

Power Key: *Agreement Is The Birthplace Of The Supernatural.*

Mary's response is one of the most beautiful statements in all of Scripture. *Luke 1:38 (KJV), And Mary said, Behold the handmaid of the Lord;* **be it unto me** *according to Thy word...* therefore, it was. Mary agreed with her purpose in life and the blessings of agreement poured out. Soon, she was singing the Magnificat: *Luke 1:48b,49, ...For behold, from now on all generations [of all ages] will call me blessed and declare me happy and to be envied! For He Who is almighty has done great things for me – and holy is His name [to be venerated in His purity, majesty and glory]!* Mary becomes the most favored of all women.

How would you like to be the most favored among all your peers? Dr. Murdock says, "One day of favor is worth a thousand days of labor." How true, because when God unlocks His favor in your life through agreement, you will never be the same! There are blessings beyond your wildest dreams awaiting when you operate in the favor of God through the power of agreement. Do not put it off. Start walking in the favor of God. Release old ways, old thought patterns and let go of the offense.

Power Key: *The Fruit Of Agreement Is Favor.*

The Mighty One desires to do great things for you and me as well. He desires to favor us all. Discern His purpose and agree with it.

Power Key: *Agreement With Your Purpose Accelerates The Fulfillment Of Your Destiny.*

When you agree with the Lord's purposes, He causes things beyond your wildest dreams to come true – even dreams not known to you. As Ephesians 3:20 (KJV) says, *"Now unto him that is able to do exceedingly abundantly above all that we ask or think..."*

Agreement with your purpose may cost you dearly. Mary had to endure the scorn of her village, the wounded misunderstanding of her husband (until he had his own angelic visitation) and carrying within her an utterly unfathomable mystery.

Coming into agreement with God means you must be willing to change. If you refuse change, you refuse His presence – and *His presence is the key to fulfillment.*

Power Key: *Refusing To Change Is Inevitably Refusing The Holy Spirit.*

Psalm 16:11 (KJV), Thou wilt show me the path of life: in thy presence is fullness of joy; at thy right hand there are pleasures forevermore.

If you agree with change, you can have the peace Psalm 119:165 (KJV) states: *"Great peace have they that love thy law, and nothing shall offend them."*

After a brief but fierce wrestling match with doubt and unbelief, Mary accepted the awesome assignment that would forever change her life. However, she did not shut herself in her room and ponder the experience for weeks. Nor did she consult with friends and neighbors on this cosmic occurrence, seeking someone who could explain what in the world was happening to her. She knew it was likely they would roll their eyes in contempt and write her off as a heretic. Never share your dreams with someone unqualified to help you fulfill them.

Mary could have reasoned like the 10 spies in the Book of Numbers, "I can't believe God expects me to give birth to a baby without even asking me." or "It's just so *unnatural*; I wish it had not happened this way."

If Mary had hung around Nazareth and attempted to go it alone, she might well have succumbed to self-pity and bitterness. Bearing the Son of God must have been an enormous burden, just as exhorting two million Israelites to enter the Promised Land must have seemed overwhelming to Joshua.

Mary's acceptance of her new found pregnancy instigated a desire to tell someone. The Bible says, Mary pondered the things which the angel shared with her and, just like any young girl excited about her news, she "went with haste" to her cousin Elizabeth's house. God knew she would not be able to share this news with just anyone; it would have to be someone who could agree with her fate. Mary did not delay or procrastinate. She immediately obeyed the inner promptings of the Holy Spirit.

Agreement brings strength and power; Mary knew she needed this. She knew the burden was too much to bear alone. God will always provide someone to agree with you.

Power Key: *As Long As There Is Someone To Agree With, There Is Always Hope For A Brighter Day.*

It is impossible to come into agreement with someone without them being present. How crucial it is that we link up with the right people. The favor of God can only be released when we come into agreement with someone else – but not just anybody.

Just as God sent Caleb to Joshua to agree with him about going into the Promised Land, centuries later, God sends Mary one to agree with.

Luke 1:39-45, And at that time Mary arose and went with haste into the hill country to a town of Judah. And she went to the house of Zachariah and, entering it, saluted Elizabeth and it occurred that when Elizabeth heard Mary's greeting, the baby leaped in her womb, and Elizabeth was filled with and controlled by the Holy Spirit. And she cried out with a loud cry, and then exclaimed, Blessed (favored of God) above all other women are you! And blessed (favored of God) is the Fruit of your womb! And how [have I deserved that this honor should] be granted to me, that the mother of my

Lord should come to me? For behold, the instant the sound of your salutation reached my ears, the baby in my womb leaped for joy. And blessed (happy, to be envied) is she who believed that there would be a fulfillment of the things that were spoken to her from the Lord.

~Agreement = Yes~

Mary had only to greet her cousin to gain her instantaneous, overjoyed readiness for agreement. Imagine the results if all God's people were so agreeable, so ready to explode "YES!" in every circumstance. Agreeable people are quick to say yes to the dreams and desires of others knowing that God will in turn do the same for them. This really is a simple principle; but self-ishness, pride and envy distort the beauty of wanting the best for others. Ephesians 6:8 says, *"Knowing that for whatever good anyone does, he will receive his reward from the Lord, whether he is slave or free."*

It is interesting to note that not only did Elizabeth immediately agree with Mary, she praised Mary for agreeing with God's purpose. *Luke 1:45 And blessed is she who believed that there would be a fulfillment of what had been spoken to her by the Lord.*

Agreeing with your purpose means believing that God is big enough to fulfill it. Psalm 138:8 says, *"The Lord will perfect that which concerns me..."* Philippians 1:6 says, *"...He Who began a good work in you will continue until the day of Jesus Christ."*

Abraham's unwavering stance of faith is a marvelous example of agreement with God.

Romans 4:18-21, [For Abraham, human reason for] hope being gone, hoped in faith that he should become the father of many nations, as he had been promised. So [numberless] shall your descendants be. He did not weaken in faith when he considered the [utter] impotence of his own body, which was as good as dead because he was about a hundred years old, or [when he considered] the barrenness of Sarah's [deadened] womb. No unbelief or distrust made him waver (doubtingly question) concerning the promise of God, but he grew strong and was empowered by faith as he gave praise and glory to God, Fully satisfied and assured that God was able and mighty to keep His word and to do what He had promised.

Power Key: ***Agreement Looks Beyond What Is And Sees What Will Be.***

God is into fulfilling destiny and purpose. In fact, He loves doing so!

Jeremiah 29:11, For I know the thoughts and plans that I have for you, says, the Lord, thoughts and plans for welfare and peace and not for evil, to give you hope in your final outcome.

God will not give you talents and dreams to torment you. Instead, He often delays the fulfillment of your purpose because He wants to shape your character through obedience. This is what transpired when Jesus, as recorded in John 10, delayed two days before going to see His dear friends Lazarus, Mary and Martha. The delay allowed doubt and unbelief to surface in the hearts of Mary and Martha.

In the case of Mary, the mother of Jesus, as soon as she came into agreement with Elizabeth, her destiny unfurled before her like a beautiful flag snapping in the wind. The Master Key of agreement unlocked the door to her destiny. Abundant life poured into her soul.

As joy and fulfillment coursed through her being, Mary poured out the prophetic Magnificat.

God has a beautiful dream, a splendid, high purpose for your life. All you have to do is come into agreement with it. He takes care of the rest.

PRAYER OF AGREEMENT:

Dear Lord, Help me to discover and come into agreement with my purpose. Help me to keep focused on my assignment and give me the willingness to change. I want to be perfectly aligned with Your Spirit. I am in agreement.

Amen

POWER KEYS:

~Agreement Is The Master Key To Anything Desired From God.
~Agreement Is The Foundation For Perpetual Prosperity.
~Satan Cannot Violate The Boundaries Of God's Will For Your Life.
~The Opportunity For Agreement Is Often But For A Moment.
~The Marriage Of Faith And Agreement Produces The

Impossible.
~Agreement Is The Birthplace Of The Supernatural.
~The Fruit Of Agreement Is Favor.
~Agreement With Your Purpose Accelerates The Fulfillment Of Your Destiny.
~Refusing To Change Is Inevitably Refusing The Holy Spirit.
~As Long As There Is Someone To Agree With, There Is Always Hope For A Brighter Day.
~Agreement Looks Beyond What Is And Sees What Will Be.

~6~

THE SHADOW OF AGREEMENT

Power Key: *Agreement Is Abiding In The Shadow Of The Most High.*

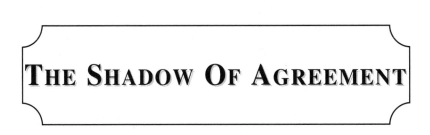hen you choose to walk in agreement, you become positioned under the Shadow of Agreement. In this realm you can walk in joy and contentment. Problems become increasingly insignificant, because you have a covering of ultimate protection. The Shadow of Agreement is the Godhead. *Psalm 63:7 (KJV), Because Thou hast been my help, therefore in the shadow of Thy wings will I rejoice.* **Everything that man desires is wrapped in agreement.** Nothing works of itself. Nothing can be accomplished without agreement. God created the entire cosmos as a whole. Everything is interconnected. Light bulbs work in concerted effort with electricity to produce light. Without the cooperation

of the sun's light, the moon would lose its glow. A car serves no purpose without a driver.

Agreement is the essence of the Godhead, because They are One. I have purposed to create an agreeable atmosphere everywhere I go. I have invested many hours with my staff creating this environment of peace and agreeability in the workplace. I have come to realize the more agreeability added to any environment creates an atmosphere for growth. In the ambiance of agreement, anything is possible, because within this climate the Holy Spirit is free to move. Furthermore, it always increases productivity and makes for a virtually stressless setting.

Power Key: *Agreement Creates The Atmosphere For Creativity.*

When the angel Gabriel spoke to Mary, he said, *"The Holy Spirit will come upon you, and the power of the Most High shall overshadow you..."*. This signifies that the Spirit of God was one level and the power of the Almighty was, yet, another level. The overshadowing was the essence of the Godhead which is agreement. When you come into agreement, there is a supernatural covering which overshadows you, much like the children of Israel were covered by the cloud of God's glory. When the people of God begin to protect and nurture this Shadow of Agreement in their lives, I believe there will be an anointing for supernatural happenings like never before.

~The Shadow, The Word And The Holy Spirit~

When this Shadow hovers over a believer who has already received the seed of God's Word and the Holy Ghost has come upon them with power, this creates a combination that will result in mighty exploits. I am convinced this is the same Shadow which accompanied the Apostle Peter and healed the sick. *Acts 5:15 (KJV) Insomuch that they brought forth the sick into the streets, and laid them on beds and couches, that at least the shadow of Peter passing by might overshadow some of them.* When the Shadow of Agreement hovers over God's people, nothing will stop the evident and much anticipated revival that the prophets prophesied.

This Shadow not only provides supernatural power for the believer, but also dispels the hordes of darkness. I am talking about the very *essence,* the very *power*, and the very *life source of Jehovah God* overshadowing you! The more you walk in agreement with your spouse, friends, colleagues, and close relationships, the more agreeable you are with your purpose. You are essentially embodying the power of God.

Power Key: *Agreement Provides Protection.*

This is where the anointing of agreement comes into its power. You do not have to fight demons or devils; they will be running from you, because of this great anointing. There is safety for those who dwell in agreement, even in the ensuing events of the last days. *Daniel 11:32, "And such as violate the covenant (agreement) he*

shall pervert and seduce with flatteries, but the people who know their God shall prove themselves strong and shall stand firm and do exploits [for God]." The antichrist will strive to lure God's people into abandoning the covenant.

Man's struggles and strains are a signal he is reaching for God's presence. Whether saved, unsaved, Christian, Buddhist, or Muslim, all of mankind is striving to get to the presence of Jehovah God. Yet, they are unwilling to go through the door; which is Jesus, the Way, the Truth and the Life. Man has a natural fascination for the presence of his Creator. Dr. Murdock says, "Everything God made, He left Himself out", so that nothing you attain will ever satisfy you. God will never give you something that will take His place.

The price of God's presence is costly. The Book of Daniel tells us, the people who know their God shall be strong and carry out great exploits. The word *know* used in this text speaks not only of perceiving and understanding; it is the same word used to describe the physical intimacy between a husband and wife. When you come into an intimacy with the presence of the Lord, you position yourself for a genesis experience.

Power Key: *Anything Cloaked In Secrecy Is Evil.*

Veiled behind the cloak of self is the Shadow of Agreement. When a believer removes the cloak and becomes intimate with the presence of the Lord, the revelation of things not seen is manifested. *I Corinthians 2:9 (KJV), "But as it is written, Eye hath not seen, nor*

ear heard, neither have entered into the heart of man, the things which God hath prepared for them that love Him. But God hath revealed them unto us by His Spirit; for the Spirit searcheth all things, yea, the deep things of God."

Power Key: *The Intimacy Of Agreement Is The Birthplace Of New Beginnings.*

When you have bared everything, when there are no secrets between you and God, you become eligible to *know* God. The intimate knowledge of God ushers you into a realm where things, which have never existed before, are birthed.

God wants to deposit the seed of His Word within believers, impregnating them with His power. The Shadow of Agreement is the incubator for the seed of the Word.

Can you imagine what Mary must have felt when she finally grasped the fact that within her was: the Anointed One, the Messiah, the Son of Jehovah God, Who was, Who is, Who is to come, the Alpha and the Omega, the Beginning and the End! The greatness of God's presence was housed within her young, frail body.

~*Mighty Exploits*~

The Church carries this same seed; every born-again believer is pregnant with the Word of God. The culmination of the seed within you empowered by the Spirit of God, the Baptizer, and the essence of agreement overshadowing you, will fulfill what the Scripture says in

Daniel 11:32, *"The people who know their God shall be strong, and carry out great exploits."*

There are things in your life that God wants you to have that you have not even dreamed of or thought of. I shared with my congregation the other day on this topic and came to the realization that we are so much more than what we see. Say to yourself right where you are, *"My life is so much more than I can see."* You are so much more than what you see in your life today! Do you want to see things you have never seen before? For example, your family may be accustomed to passionless marriages. Your ability to walk in the agreement coupled with the Holy Spirit and the Word can cause your marriage to be the most exciting one your family has ever seen. ***Anything you want is already in existence***, except that it is not yet made visible to you.

Power Key: *The Secrets Of The Lord Are Revealed To The Sweet Worshipper.*

Psalm 25:14, The secret [of the sweet, satisfying companionship] of the Lord have they who fear (revere and worship) Him, and He will show them His covenant and reveal to them its [deep, inner] meaning.

There are things that have not yet been revealed that are hidden behind the Shadow of Agreement. The key to unlocking these mysteries is in your worship. Not just any worship will do. God is very specific, in this case, He is calling for "sweet" worship. ***Sweet worship is simply a heart absent of offense and filled with gratitude.*** Are you ready to unlock the unimaginable?

The Scripture in I Corinthians begins by saying, "Eye hath not seen..." Your eyes have not yet seen *"things"* which you may or may not have petitioned of the Lord, but that does not mean they do not exist. Jesus told Mary and Martha, the sisters of Lazarus, in John 11:40, *"Did I not tell you and promise you that if you would believe and rely on Me, you would see the glory of God?"* The only prerequisite to seeing is believing. All you have to do to see those things, which are not yet seen, is to believe.

Mark 9:23, And Jesus said [you say to Me], if You can do anything? [Why,] all things can be (are possible) to him who believes!

I know you are probably thinking I am not aware of the circumstances that are surrounding you at this very moment. That is just it, when you agree and stay in the agreement, the action of your agreement creates a Shadow of God's glory over your life and your circumstances. Imagine yourself standing before your enemies and with great astonishment and bewilderment they begin to retreat. That is what will happen every time you choose agreement, your enemy will see the glory of God overshadowing you and will flee.

In the multiple centuries represented in the Scriptures, there is no other account comparable to the events of Acts Chapter Two. There is no other incident or demonstration of the supernatural like the day of Pentecost. Have you ever heard of the Holy Spirit descending upon people with the evidence of cloven tongues of fire on their heads as in the day of Pentecost? Never! It was the birthplace of a brand new occurrence never before experienced.

May I pose before you, there are things in the Spirit, things in the realm of the unimaginable that man cannot conceive. *Eye hath not seen, nor ear heard...*, but through the act of agreement God's people can unlock something that this world has never before seen. You have the power to unlock something that has never before existed! You could be the Ezekiel that unlocks the resurrection power to awaken a desperately lost and dying world. It could be something so supernatural that even the psychics, witches, and warlocks would have to declare, "The God of the Christians is the true God!"

I can only imagine what it would be like to stand before several thousand people operating in agreement, agreeing to simply worship the Lord. A great anointing would be released, unlike any the Church has ever experienced.

Worship is the fragrance and aroma that causes God to pursue those whom He has distinguished as the recipients of His glory. *The people who know their God...* shall become pregnant and, after a season, they will begin to show what happened in the secret place.

John 14:2 states *"In My Father's house are many rooms..."* How will the Church abide in the same house for all eternity with people's disputatious demeanors? Have you ever shared a room with a group of people for any length of time? It seems like everyone becomes quite contentious and disagreeable. Jesus said in John 14:1-2, *"Let not your heart be troubled: ye believe in God, believe also in Me. In My Father's house are many mansions: if it were not so, I would have told you. I go to*

prepare a place for you. And If I go and prepare a place for you, I will come again and receive you unto Myself; that where I am, there ye may be also."

Within the domain of God, there are many rooms, many mansions. Jesus makes the statement: *"...that where I am, there ye may be also."* **There are secret places in God that can only be discovered by tapping into the patterns of the whole – God's presence.** When you come into close proximity with the fullness of the Godhead, you will discover worlds unknown.

PRAYER OF AGREEMENT:

Dear Lord, I thank You for Your protection. I thank You for Your covering and for the things You have hidden away for me, just behind the Shadow. I will not be moved by the mystery of a Shadow, even the Shadow of death. I will welcome it with joy knowing it carries the unimaginable.

Amen

POWER KEYS:

~Agreement Is Abiding In The Shadow Of The Most High.
~Agreement Provides Protection
~Agreement Creates The Atmosphere For Creativity.
~Anything Cloaked In Secrecy Is Evil.
~The Intimacy Of Agreement Is The Birthplace Of New Beginnings.
~The Secrets Of The Lord Are Revealed To The Sweet Worshipper.

~7~

THE INTIMACY OF AGREEMENT

Power Key: *The Intimacy Of Agreement Is The Birthplace For New Beginnings.*

American culture encourages self-sufficiency. No one person can be everything, but every now and then, everybody tries. "Super" Moms and Dads wear themselves out by working high-pressured careers, carting kids to an endless string of activities and working to maintain an ever-growing pile of possessions.

Everyone can attest, that often at the end of a hectic day, feelings of loneliness, exhaustion and emptiness seem to be the only rewards for back breaking toil. Even a day packed with people can seem empty and unfulfilling if it lacks the Intimacy of Agreement.

As was discussed earlier in this book, agreement is

the essence of the Father, the Son and the Holy Spirit. Any day that goes by without drinking deeply of the divine elixir of agreement will result in an unfruitful, unfulfilling day. You may perform a great deed at your job or in your community, but if agreement is not in the vanguard of your attitude, your work will be in vain.

Power Key: ***When You Move Beyond Your Fear, You Are Made Free!***

The Intimacy of Agreement is found in holding nothing back. Intimacy requires vulnerability, risk and passion. There is nothing more perturbing than a passionless man or woman. It gives the impression of being spineless and without direction. The Intimacy of Agreement provides freedom from fear within relationships. There is a difference between honoring someone's passion and sharing their passion. Intimacy moves you past simply honoring or admiring passion; it engrafts you to that passion.

Either you flow in agreement or you choose not to. There are no degrees of agreement. You are either agreeable or disagreeable. You are either yielded to the Lord or offended.

Not to beat a dead horse (although sometimes believers act like dead horses), but offense is what creates the terrible isolation that pervades our culture.

Power Key: ***Offense Creates Isolation.***

People who totally isolate themselves are offended people. They shun close relationships, because deep down, they do not want to submit themselves to anyone. They choose not to agree. Agreement is a choice! Proverbs 18:1 says, *"He who isolates himself rages against all sound wisdom."*

Consider a few of the tyrants of the last century: Hitler, Stalin, and Mao. They all eventually flamed out, dying self-destructive or lonely, paranoid deaths. They tried to be everything; they tried, in essence, to be God. However, they were not God and in the end reaped a horrible harvest of corruption and death. They were not in agreement with anyone except themselves.

A friend of mine jokes that when he is struggling to understand and sympathize with his wife, he sometimes wishes he could have married himself. Then he would always be in effortless agreement with his spouse!

Alas, agreement is not that easy. As was discussed in earlier chapters, agreement will cost you, your pride, your time, and ultimately everything. Like Jesus in the Garden of Gethsemane, agreement means laying down your will. They are wonderful, yet, terrible words: *"Not my will, but Thy will be done."* That is the cost of agreement.

Power Key: *Agreement Is The Binding Force Behind Any Successful Relationship.*

God likes relationships. He made you for the purpose of having intimate relationships with others. In addition, the reward is intimacy with God and intimacy with one another.

I believe this is a key reason why He endues power to groups of two or more who can agree. Certainly, God hears you when you pray sincerely by yourself. Nevertheless, something incredible happens when "two or more" pray together. In Leviticus 26:8, God reveals a little of His mathematics, "one can set 1,000 to flight, but two can set 10,000 to flight". Logically, in this equation, one plus one should put two thousand to flight not 10,000. Nevertheless, with "God's Math", if two put 10,000 to flight, it stands to reason that 3, 15, or 1,000 will put a vast host to flight.

Consider Gideon and his band of 300 in the Book of Judges. The army opposing them was too numerous to count. Yet, the unity, boldness and agreement of the little group, which was approximately the size of an average church in America today, destroyed a vast army! Think of the mighty works that could be done if each church in America became unified and agreeable!

~David And Jonathan Agree~

The story of David and Jonathan in I Samuel is one of the Bible's most beautiful illustrations of the Intimacy of Agreement.

I Samuel 18:1-4, When David had finished speaking to Saul, the soul of Jonathan was knit with the soul of David, and Jonathan loved him as his own life. Saul took David that day and would not let him return to his father's house. Then Jonathan made a covenant with David, because he loved him as his own life. And Jonathan stripped himself of the robe that was on him and gave it to David, and his armor, even his sword, his bow, and his girdle.

David had loyally served King Saul, Jonathan's father, for many months. Saul's disobedience and rebellion eventually stripped him of his anointing as king. That anointing was then placed upon David. Saul grew jealous and paranoid and sought to kill David. At great personal risk, Jonathan befriends David and helps him survive Saul's murderous rages.

In the verses above, Jonathan lays down his armor, in effect declaring, "See, I won't hurt you. Here are my weapons and armor. I am in agreement with you."

The cost for Jonathan was enormous. Jonathan, the heir to Saul's throne, was in essence giving up his right to be king.

I have encountered many people in my 18 years of ministry whose personal dreams, visions and goals have been too great to lay down. Does your dream seem to be greater than your mentor's dream? Is your vision for reaching others larger than the vision of your church? Perhaps, you feel more equipped for greatness than those in authority over you. Is it in your character, as it was with Jonathan, to lay down the scepter to your kingdom to embrace someone else's dream? Jonathan recognized the Lord's anointing upon David, agreed with it and honored it by protecting David.

- *Agreement chooses not to hurt the one you are agreeing with.*
- *Agreement seeks to protect the one you are agreeing with.*
- *Agreement provides a wonderful sense of security.*

~The Network Of Agreement~

No matter what happens, you have the assurance of knowing those in agreement with you are on your side. You walk about confidently, always aware you have allies walking beside you in the Intimacy of Agreement.

Agreement extends beyond the relationships with which you are personally involved. If you will enter into prayer, you can tap into a vast network of people all over the world who are in the same agreement with you. In the Book of Ephesians, Paul admonishes the reader to "pray at all times for all believers." It is crucial that believers carry out this command. An unknown believer, whom you may never meet, may be desperately waiting for your prayer, for you to agree with him or her on a desperate matter.

Through the new covenant agreement as detailed in Hebrews 8:8-9, you have the confidence of knowing there is an entire network of believers connected to you in agreement. What an awesome thought! When you pray according to the "will", "testament" or "agreement", you are joined by the millions of saints whose names are also found in God's "contract" of blessings. Think of it as a step up from the World Wide Web. You are connected to the UWW (Universal Wide Web). Get connected today; come into agreement with another believer and stay in the agreement.

PRAYER OF AGREEMENT:

Lord, I thank You that through my worship, I am unlocking the unimaginable. Help me to lay down my desires to help someone else fulfill theirs. I know that intimacy in agreement involves vulnerability and risk. I am willing to take that risk. I know that what I make happen for others, You will make happen for me. In Your Name I pray.

Amen

POWER KEYS:

~The Intimacy Of Agreement Is The Birthplace Of New Beginnings.
~When You Move Beyond Your Fear, You Are Made Free!
~Offense Creates Isolation.
~Agreement Is The Binding Force Behind Any Successful Relationship.

~8~

Agreement And Worship

Power Key: *Unquenchable Worship Is The Wine Of Addiction To His Presence.*

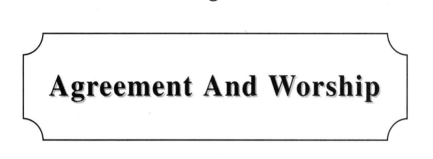 magine for a moment that you are an artist's canvas. Your life is difficult. First, the painter coats you with sticky, white goo of gesso, softening you up for the paint. Then you are nailed to a board and stretched to your outer limits, every fiber in you screaming for relief. Finally, the paint is applied and scraped off, reapplied and re-scraped off, reapplied . . .

Dreading another "re-scrape", you suddenly cry out, "God, give me a break!" The truth is you do not need a break. Rather, what you need is to be *broken*.

I recently wrote a worship song called "Special Moments in His Presence" which describes the delicate tension between the beauty of worship and the inherent darkness in human flesh:

"Special moments in Your presence,
Breaking down my defenses,
Special moments in Your presence,
I'm seeking You with all my senses.
I want to know You with my heart,
I want to know You with all my soul.
Please tell me where do I begin,
Where do I start?"

Power Key: ***Worship Dismantles Defenses Making***
One Teachable.

Where to start... It must begin with Worship. Like prayer, Worship is a powerful expression of agreement, because it fosters humility while lifting your inner man. James 4:10 urges, *"Humble yourself in the sight of the Lord, and He will lift you up."* To worship God is to agree with God that He is mighty, holy, awesome and worthy of praise. On the other hand, to Worship God is to agree with God about your limitations, sin and desperate need for redemption. Agreeing with God in Worship breaks down defenses which are secretly erected within the soul to protect pride, wounds, shame and ultimately offense. Worship washes away all the self-destructiveness of pride and offense. It takes one back to the beginning, to spiritual nakedness. It creates a willingness to start from scratch with God with no presuppositions or pride. Like the crushed and repentant Job the soul cries, *"Behold, I am insignificant; what can I reply to Thee?"*

Power Key: *True Worship Reveals The Character Of A Person, Thus, Worship Is Integrity.*

Alternatively, one whispers, like the astonished David as he stared at the sweeping expanse of stars:

Psalm 8:1-4, O Lord, our Lord, how excellent (majestic and glorious) is Your name in all the earth! You have set your glory on [or above] the heavens. Out of the mouths of babes and unweaned infants you have established strength because of your foes that you might silence the enemy and the avenger. When I view and consider your heavens, the work of your fingers, the moon and the stars, which you have ordained and established, what is man that You are mindful of him, and the son of [earthborn] man that you care for him?

God does not reveal the finiteness of man to make man feel crummy, worthless and insignificant. He elevated both Job and David; they had to go *low* to be lifted *high*. They had to agree through Worship about God's greatness and their own finiteness. God desires to reveal glimpses of His greatness and allows the ensuing thrill to enlarge the vision of what He can do through His people.

~*Framing Your World*~

God framed the worlds with His Word. *Hebrews 11:3 (KJV), Through faith we understand that the worlds were framed by the word of God, so that things which are seen were not made of things which do appear.*

God desperately desires to enlarge His people's vision and enlarge the frames that encompass the canvas of their lives. He does not want them to spend their whole lives in tiny 3-inch by 5-inch frames when His plan calls for filling out a magnificent, gold-gilded, 12 foot by 12 foot museum-masterpiece frame.

Many believers have learned a great deal from the Word of God, but have only a small 5-inch by 7-inch frame to hold the canvas of life. Here the Artist Himself embellishes their black and white world. He (Holy Spirit) splashes brilliant colors on the dismal dreariness of their canvases and awakens the sleeping champion within. An enormous vision cannot fit in a small frame. As you grow in agreement – learning to submit to one another, to the man of God, to God Himself – you increase the size of your frame.

To enlarge the vision of what God wants to accomplish through you, you must learn to WAR everyday. The type of warfare the Church has become so accustomed to in the last two decades has been from the vantage point of defeating the devil. **Warfare is not a daily battle against Satan.** What is the purpose of fighting a defeated foe?

~*Lovers Not Fighters*~

The purpose of the Church is not for warfare; it is for Worship. God's Word declares that He created people for His pleasure. In other words, He desires believers to be lovers not fighters; they are called to be worshippers not warriors. The battle is not against a defeated foe; it is against the nature of the accuser that reveals itself through man's offensive attitudes and actions. Jesus' purpose was to destroy the works of the devil.

I John 3:8b, …for this purpose was the Son of God manifest, to destroy the works of the devil. If Jesus' assignment on the earth was for the destruction of Satan, why should the believers expend their energy attempting to defeat the devil? Was Jesus redemptive work on the cross not sufficient for defeating Satan?

The purpose of the Church is to please God. How does the Church please Him? Through faith. ***True faith is worshipping, even when the fulfillment of a request made to God has not manifested.*** The duty and purpose of the Church is to worship the Lord. Psalm 65 states, *"To You belongs silence (the submissive wonder of reverence which bursts forth into praise) and praise is due and fitting to You, O God, in Zion; and to You shall the vow be performed. Blessed (happy, fortunate, to be envied) is the man whom You choose and cause to come near, that he may dwell in Your courts! We shall be satisfied with the goodness of Your house, Your holy temple."*

The Scripture says, *"Blessed, happy, to be envied is the man whom God chooses and calls into His courts."* The courts of the Lord are filled with praise. When you have a disagreeable attitude, you have nothing praiseworthy to speak. I am not referring to speaking a positive word to offset a negative one. Do not underestimate or miscalculate the power and the effectiveness of agreement. The difference between speaking a positive word and walking in agreement is the positive word requires no agreement. If you have been chosen of God and called into His courts of praise, you must bare the mark of a worshipper.

To walk in agreement is to have an attitude of

praise regardless of the surrounding circumstances. You must abide in the courts of the Lord no matter what you are going through. The courtship of the Lord is available to anyone while the Worship of the Lord is exclusively for those with an offense-free heart. Remember, Agreement is the absence of offense.

I shared with you, in Chapter One, the dream of the Father was to have a people who would Worship in spirit and in truth through song. The weapon God has given you to combat the works of darkness is to simply Worship the Lord. However, you must understand that Worship with offense in the heart is nothing more than ritualism. How sad, God created His people for relationship through Worship, yet, many of them are so exhausted from fighting devils that they have no joy or energy left for Worship.

Are you tired of fighting devils? Allow me to share with you a different concept of war against your enemies. *Why not try worshipping your way to victory?* Give God your very best and quit giving Him the leftovers. WAR against the works of darkness!

There are three levels of Worship that you must learn to master:

1. **Worship And Rejoice.** You must grow to the point where you care about God's presence in your life more than anything. His presence must become your daily obsession. The agreement of worship blossoms when you are desperate for *Him* and *not* for His blessings. You must grow to where you desire His presence continually – not the quick fix of Holy Spirit hocus-pocus. When

you are content with God's presence, you can move on to the next level of WAR.

2. **Wisdom And Revelation.** When your heart has been softened and opened by Worship, you are in a much better position to receive deposits of wisdom and instruction from God. When you have been humbled by Worship over a long period of time, when God *knows* you truly are His, He can trust you with an increased understanding of the supernatural. When you become mature and wise, God can then move you into the third step of WAR.

3. **Wealth And Riches.** Everyone wants this step first. "Give me the blessings, Lord, I can handle it!" "You can trust me!" you exclaim. Hah! Few believers make it to this step in the full maturation of agreement, because they are unwilling to do the humbling, hard work of steps one and two. Only the truly wise, agreeable person can handle the huge responsibility of wealth and riches.

God wants you to be able to keep wealth in perspective. This is highly difficult. Jesus used some of His strongest, most colorful language to express this dilemma.

Matthew 19:24, Again I tell you, it is easier for a camel to go through the eye of a needle than for a rich man to go into the kingdom of heaven.

Matthew 6:24, No one can serve two masters; for either he will hate the one and love the other, or he will stand by and be devoted to the one and despise and be against the other. You cannot serve God and mammon

(deceitful riches, money, possessions, or whatever is trusted in).

~*Prosperity And His Presence*~

The error of much prosperity teaching today is that it teaches people how to access God's hand of provision, but not how to properly access His presence. I believe the Church is in a position, through the teaching of prosperity, where it can appropriate just about anything it desires. That is a powerful statement and very true. God has revealed the road to His treasures to many, but few have inquired about the Giver.

I am a firm believer in the teaching of the laws of sowing and reaping. One of the books I am writing is on the subject of Sowing for the Unimaginable. However, before I can share my secrets for success in living, I am compelled to share with you about the Giver. Too many Christians are blessed with money, cars, high-powered careers and houses, but they leave God at the altar. There is not one thing you own today that God did not provide for you.

God left himself out of everything, so that His people would always reach for Him. It does not matter how much money a person can amass; there will always be a cry for more. For more of what? It is not more money, cars or houses that the soul craves; it is a natural propensity from within reaching for the Creator. The Church must learn that His presence is our most valued treasure.

"Lord you are more precious than silver.
Lord you are more costly than gold.
Lord you are more beautiful than diamonds,
And nothing that I desire compares with You." -Author unknown

The Bible is clear; God is a jealous God. He will tolerate no rivals. His ways are not our ways, but His way is a path of splendor and glory; it is brimming with precious fruit, precious people, and precious surprises. The favor of God! His will is a perfect will, a broad place where delight can be found. Nevertheless, this broad place must first be rid of the rivals and idols that would steal away your wholehearted devotion to God.

Deuteronomy 7:1-4 (KJV), When the Lord thy God shall bring thee into the land whither thou goest to possess it, and hath cast out many nations before thee, the Hittites, and the Girgashites, and the Amorites, and the Canaanites, and the Perizzites, and the Hivites, and the Jebusites, seven nations greater and mightier than thou; and when the Lord thy God shall deliver them before thee, thou shalt smite them, and utterly destroy them; thou shalt make no covenant with them, nor show mercy unto them: neither shalt thou make marriages with them; thy daughter thou shalt not give unto his son, nor his daughter shalt thou take unto thy son. For they will turn away thy son from following Me, that they may serve other gods, so will the anger of the Lord be kindled against you, and destroy you suddenly.

God's concern was not that the seven nations, already dwelling in Canaan, would rise up and repossess the land, driving the Israelites back into the wilderness.

God's seemingly, brutal stipulation, about utterly destroying these pagan peoples, arose from His intimate acquaintance with the fickle, wicked, human heart. God knew that if His people mixed with the Hittites, Girgashites, Amorites and the other "ites", they would draw the hearts of His people away from worshipping Him. When you come into agreement with your purpose, it will drive out people who may be potential obstacles to your focus. You must be willing to lay those relationships down.

Is there something drawing you from truly worshipping the Lord? Is there unresolved sin hindering you from worshipping freely? The Psalmist wrote, *"Search me O God, try me and know my thoughts. See if there be any wickedness in me."*

It has become quite evident to me why the Church has lost its ability to worship. As you will read in a later chapter about broken covenant, it will become more apparent to you. ***God is calling His Church back to worship.***

There is something powerful and mighty connected to your Worship, or Satan's focus would not be directed at keeping the Church from worshipping.

The Body of Christ has no problem with the idea of "courting the Lord". *Psalm 100:4 (KJV), Enter into His gates with thanksgiving, and into His courts with praise: be thankful unto Him, and bless His name.* Praise comes easily because it requires no intimacy or vulnerability. According to Scripture, even rocks can praise Him.

Power Key: *Worship Incites God's Desire Toward Us.*

I do not know of too many believers who fully understand the power of true Worship. A grateful heart filled with Worship leads to the mercy of God which is the *favor* of God. *(More on unlocking the favor of God in Chapter 11)*

You must also drive out the "ites" of offense and disagreement in your heart – the sin that prevents us from entering into true Worship of God.

God desires your true Worship above all else. He is passionate about connecting with His people on the spiritual plane of Worship. He knows this is the only thing that can satisfy the soul. True Worship continues to exalt and enjoy God whether the blessings are showering down or whether they are nonexistent. Worship is the revealer of a man's faith. Faith is worshipping God, even when you do not receive the fulfillment of what you have petitioned.

Power Key: *Worship Is Faith Without Visible Fulfillment Of The Promise.*

God is seeking out worshippers, people who will Worship Him in spirit and in truth. The woman at the well, in John 4, discovered true Worship when she beheld the glory of God through Christ. Jesus gently led her toward true Worship and her life was never the same. He embraced the agreeable factor and reached someone that otherwise would have never been touched, because of her nationality. A woman, who was familiar with the ritualism of Worship through religion, had an encounter with the object of true Worship, Jesus, and was made whole.

Power Key: *The Revolution Of Worship Is A Revolt Against Crippling Tradition.*

John 4:19-24 (KJV), Our fathers worshipped in this mountain; and ye say, that in Jerusalem is the place where men ought to worship. Jesus said unto her, Woman, believe me, the hour cometh, when ye shall neither in this mountain, nor yet at Jerusalem, worship the Father. Ye worship ye know not what: we know what we worship: for salvation is of the Jews. But the hour cometh, and now is, when the true worshippers shall worship the Father in spirit and in truth: for the Father seeketh such to worship Him. God is a Spirit: and they that worship Him must worship Him in spirit and truth.

It is crucial to note that God is *seeking* worshippers. He desires worshippers with all His heart. The word seeketh in the Greek is "zeteo" which means to require; a demand of something due; a search for something hidden; an urgent need; ask, demand, inquire, understand.

Allow me to paraphrase John 4:21, *"The Father is requiring, demanding of something due to Him, searching for something hidden, because of His urgent need, for worshippers who will worship in Spirit and in truth."* God has an urgent need for true worshippers. **The posture and attitude of a worshipper is a direct reflection of the eminence of the One he worships.** Unquestionably, the attitude of a person being presented to a dignitary is of prime importance, because attitudes govern actions.

Power Key: *Actions Are Governed By Attitudes.*

Even a child understood the magnitude of approaching a dignitary with the proper attitude. The little boy carrying the two fish and five loaves of bread, no doubt, was on his way home carefully following his mother's instructions. He was probably carrying his family's provision for the entire week. A most amazing thing happened. From deep within, this young lad felt Jesus beckoning him. Worship is a call from deep within to give God your everything.

Power Key: *The Enemy Of Worship Is Offense.*

The Father is seeking people with the right attitude of worship. Worship cannot freely flow from the heart of a person filled with offense. The Book of James says, *"A spring doesn't gush fresh water one day and brackish the next."* Worship without integrity is impossible!

To Worship God is to agree with God that one must put to death the secret aspiration to be our own gods and simply be sons of God. Pride and offense make true worship impossible.

Romans 8:12-14 (KJV), So then brethren, we are under obligation, not to the flesh, to live according to the flesh – for if you are living according to the flesh, you must die; but if by the Spirit you are putting to death the deeds of the body, you will live. For all who are being led by the Spirit of God, these are sons of God.

PRAYER OF AGREEMENT:

Dear Jesus, Help me to be broken before You. I want to awaken the sleeping champion within me, that You see. I Worship You from my heart and I thank You for leading me into a new understanding of Worship.

Amen

POWER KEYS:

~Unquenchable Worship Is The Wine Of Addiction To His Presence.
~Worship Dismantles Defenses Making One Teachable.
~True Worship Reveals The Character Of A Person, Thus, Worship Is Integrity.
~Worship Incites God's Desire Toward Us.
~Worship Is Faith Without Visible Fulfillment Of The Promise.
~The Revolution Of Worship Is A Revolt Against Crippling Tradition.
~Actions Are Governed By Attitudes.
~The Enemy Of Worship Is Offense.

~9~

THE ATTITUDE OF AGREEMENT

Power Key: *An Attitude Of Agreement Affords Endless Possibilities.*

reate in me a clean heart, O God, and renew a right, persevering, and steadfast spirit within me. (Psalm 51:10) The word "spirit" refers to one's attitude. It is vitally important to keep the right spirit or frame of mind if your purpose is to remain in agreement. Your attitude affects your personality and your personality was designed by God to assist you in carrying out your assignment. *Attitude is everything!*

Power Key: *Attitude Determines The Kind Of People You Will Attract.*

I come from a family of seven children and no two of us are alike. Although we have the same mother and father, our personalities are completely different. Someone once said, some people are thinkers and some are feelers, some are cheerleaders and some are players, but life requires both. Your attitude will either enhance your personality or it will kill it.

There are those who are highly qualified for certain jobs with skills abounding, but a disagreeable attitude neutralizes their worth. In the kingdom of God, the person with the right attitude is not the one with confidence, but rather the one with a humble spirit. *Humility is not self-degradation; rather, it is the act of elevating someone else.* To have an agreeable spirit is to have the Spirit of Christ's humility.

Power Key: *Attitude Dictates Promotion Or Demotion*

A wrong attitude can hinder your spiritual development. You cannot accept that Jesus is the Messiah without the Holy Spirit, neither can you agree that the Holy Spirit is Who He says He is without an agreeable attitude. A wrongful attitude will dissuade you from believing the truth. It eradicates faith and disqualifies you from eternal life. Your attitude is synonymous with your spirit. An agreeable disposition requires ongoing maintenance.

Power Key: *Attitudes Are Governed By Mindsets.*

Noah purposed in his heart he would not come out

of the agreement with God. The rest of the world was reveling in their evil while Noah patiently carried out his assignment.

It matters not who comes and goes in your life. Whether those around you remain faithful to their agreement, you must decide today that you are not coming out of the agreement. Repeat this to yourself, *"I refuse to come out of the agreement."*

It is quite evident that Noah was a man with an agreeable spirit. Anyone who steadfastly remains focused on building an ark, when the world has never experienced the phenomenon of rain, has a champion attitude. A common conjecture here would be that Noah received much ridicule from the people around him. Yet, with every remark hurled at him, he only became more determined in fulfilling his purpose.

Joshua 1:6, Be strong (confident) and of good courage, for you shall cause this people to inherit the land which I swore to their fathers to give them. There are things in your future that God has already purposed for you to have. To be qualified as a recipient, you must be strong and courageous. I believe there is another level of blessing wrapped in favor and God wants you to have it. When a person enters the prime of life, it is known as the best years of their life. Yet, this is where most people stop. You must choose to go further. Regardless of how great your victories and how high up the ladder of success you have climbed, ***there is more***! Living in agreement aligns you with the realm of the Holy Spirit that ushers you into the level of the unimaginable. If you have reached the prime of your life, or if you have already passed it, prepare yourself for a second go at it.

Only be strong and courageous...

Keep focused, fulfill your vows to the Lord and stay in agreement.

Power Key: *Purpose Eliminates Distractions.*

When you make a vow to the Lord, you have bound yourself to that agreement regardless of any problems that may arise in your personal life. In a marriage, the vows are not optional; they are commitments of the heart that two people promise to carry out. They are not based on reciprocity; instead, they are based on unconditional love. Agreement is a matter of the heart, not lip service. It is based on your will and not your emotion.

Power Key: *The Evidence Of Faithfulness Is Longevity.*

Noah's perseverance finally paid off. More than 100 years after his initial agreement with God, his ship finally sailed.

Genesis 6:8, But Noah found grace (favor) in the eyes of the Lord. Obedience to the agreement produced Godly favor for Noah and his family, and they alone survived the great flood. *Genesis 6:5, The Lord saw that the wickedness of man was great in the earth, and that every imagination and intention of all human thinking was only evil continually.* The whole of the earth's population, save Noah and his family, were suffering from conscious-less mindsets. Their negligent attitudes cost them their place on Noah's Luxury Cruise Liner and ultimately their lives. An entire planet was annihilated because of their disagreeable attitudes.

Building an ark was a brand new experience for Noah. With no help from any of his neighbors, he stood alone as a blameless, righteous man, empowered and energized by his agreement with God.

Power Key: *A Poor Attitude Always Results In Loss.*

The Scripture says that he walked in habitual fellowship with the Lord. The strength of agreement lies solely in a partner's willingness to walk side by side with the agreeing party. *Beyond verbal commitment, agreement is a journey reserved for the dedicated.*

God gave Noah dominion over every living creature based on his obedience to the agreement. *Genesis 9:1,2, And God pronounced a blessing upon Noah and his sons and said to them, Be fruitful and multiply and fill the earth. And the fear of you and the dread and terror of you shall be upon every beast of the land, every bird of the air, all that creeps upon the ground, and upon all the fish of the sea; they are delivered into your hand.* Remember, Noah was in habitual fellowship with God. He was a worshipper. Many teachers in the Body of Christ are capitalizing on the power of dominion. Before you can operate in the dominion of the Word, you must understand worship. You too, must nurture a habitual relationship of worship with the Father.

Power Key: *Dominion Without Agreement Is Like Fighting A Battle Without A Weapon.*

God gave Noah everything! I mentioned earlier that everything you desire is wrapped up in agreement.

Noah's persistence in obeying God's instruction not only rewarded him with salvation from the impending flood, but it became the ransom for all of creation. God's rewards are far reaching; the favor of Noah's agreement extended to his sons and ultimately to every living creature. The perpetuity of life itself was uncertain; it hinged on Noah's obedience.

Power Key: *The Force Of Agreement Is Obedience.*

There are people who have impressive ability, but poor attitude. *The difference between attitude and ability is: Ability asks, "Can you?" Attitude asks, "Will you?"* Your attitude is a result of your choices. Any negative patterns you permit will be perpetuated.

If I allow my children to talk back to me today, they will talk back to me tomorrow; it becomes their lifestyle. What kind of attitude are you conceding to? I am not referring to a mere self-esteem problem; I am talking about a problem with your integrity.

At the heart of agreement is humility. Too many people focus on their weaknesses, instead of their strengths, resulting in low self-esteem. There is probably not a day that goes by when you look in the mirror and find something disagreeable about yourself. Maybe your nose is too big, or your hair is not the right color. The only way to correct a poor self-evaluation is to see yourself as God sees you. Your attitude should never take its form and shape from experiences. It must be patterned on what God's Word says about you.

Power Key: *The Attitude Of Agreement Is Submission.*

Agree with the Master's blueprint for your life.
Changing your attitude when you get off course is a
twofold process.

First, you confess your distasteful attitude to God
asking Him for help. Second, declare the Word of God
over your circumstances.

When you have weathered a difficult season in
your life, instead of conforming to the negative, look for
the hand of God. He is there in the ashes of your fiery
furnace. *Isaiah 43:2b, When you walk through the fire,*
you will not be burned or scorched, nor will the flame
kindle upon you.

Shadrach, Meshach and Abednego qualify as
poster children for being thrown in the fiery furnace of
their circumstances. These three remained committed to
the call of God on their lives. They stood for what they
believed in the midst of an entire city's bewitchment by
its own ruler. Regardless of the imperious orders handed
to them by the court to worship the golden image, these
three remained agreed. The standard of music, established by popular demand, dictated the form of worship.
The Bible describes the scene with everyone bowing
down to the image. Like robots, the people went down
oblivious to the dooming consequences.

As in a typical rock fest, the music was loud and
the crowd was entranced by the image before them. Yet,
three men operating in agreement (and I don't mean three

men in tights) stood and shouted praises to their God. These men were no cowards to say the least. They became spectacles before an entire nation, violating the customs of the day.

They risked public humiliation with the damning consequence of a fiery furnace. Still, they lifted up their voice with triumphant praise.

What do you suppose would have happened if Shadrach, Meshach and Abednego had erupted in disagreement? This story would have ended with the tale of the three "roasted hotheaded hotdogs" who could not find the agreeable factor.

Instead, in the midst of their fiery trials, through the power of agreement, they submitted to their fate.

Power Key: *Agreement In The Midst Of Your Struggle Is A Step On The Road To Wisdom.*

God always makes a way of escape. He is a master builder who can make pathways, doorways and exits in the midst of entrapment. His wisdom is your exit from trouble.

Amidst the lapping flames of their hell, captured like hunted animals by their enemies, a Member of the Godhead makes a command appearance and gloriously liberates the three valiant Hebrew men.

There is never a situation, problem or circumstance that you cannot handle when you maintain a right attitude.

Power Key: *The Attitude Of Agreement Is Humility.*

Like the three fireballs of faith and the unsinkable Noah, you must take on an ethos: an attitude of determination, passion, and dedication. This is the product of an agreeable attitude.

Except you take on the attitude of agreement and position yourself in a progressive mindset, you will not be able to see the fourth man in the fiery furnace with you. You will not be able to receive the revelation of the following chapter.

Power Key: *The Mastery Of Agreement Is Found In Your Decision To Become A Willing Participant.*

PRAYER OF AGREEMENT:

Almighty God, You have ordered and numbered my footsteps. I thank You that I am at the right place at the right time. Regardless of my circumstances, I know You are with me. In the midst of my fiery furnace, You are there!

Amen

POWER KEYS:

~An Attitude Of Agreement Affords Endless Possibilities.
~Attitude Determines The Kind Of People You Will Attract.
~Attitude Dictates Promotion Or Demotion.
~Attitudes Are Governed By Mindsets.
~Actions Are Governed By Attitude.

~Purpose Eliminates Distractions.
~The Evidence Of Faithfulness Is Longevity.
~A Poor Attitude Always Results In Loss.
~Dominion Without Agreement Is Like Fighting A Battle Without A Weapon.
~The Force Of Agreement Is Obedience.
~The Attitude Of Agreement Is Submission.
~Agreement In The Midst Of Your Struggle Is A Step On The Road To Wisdom.
~The Attitude Of Agreement Is Humility.
~The Mastery Of Agreement Is Found In Your Decision To Become A Willing Participant.

~10~

THE CIRCLE OF AGREEMENT

Power Key: *Agreement Is The Foundation Of All Existence.*

greement is the connectivity of the Godhead; therefore, it is the foundation of all existence. Try to imagine God the Father, the Son and the Holy Ghost without agreement. It is impossible! Imagine science without molecules. Again, impossible! Now, imagine the Body of Christ without agreement. Absolutely impossible!

*I John 5:7,8, So there are three witnesses in heaven: the Father, the Word and the Holy Spirit, and these three are One; and there are three witnesses on the earth: the Spirit, the water, and the blood; and these three [are in **unison**; their testimony coincides].*

Everything that exists is governed by the principle of three. God and man are both trichotomous beings.

The world in which we live is three-dimensional governed by three forces: electromagnetic force, force of gravity and nuclear force.

Kevin J. Conner states in his book, Interpreting The Symbols and Types, the Scriptural interpretation of the number three is: the Godhead, divine completeness and perfect testimony.

In the Old Testament, the acceptable sacrifice was brought before the Lord three times a year. There were three different kinds of feasts. Three is the number of completion. Can you see a pattern taking shape here? While the Power of Agreement is released through two people agreeing; when you agree with the Holy Spirit you move into the Anointing of Agreement.

~Correction From The Lord~

Three days and three nights Jonah spent in the belly of a whale. His journey to Nineveh was three days. Ananias died within three hours of lieing to the Holy Spirit; his wife, Sapphira died within three hours of his death. Peter denied Christ three times. Paul was blind for three days. Moses stretched out his hand and for three days a thick darkness covered the land of Egypt. He was hidden away by his mother for three months.

~Witnesses~

I Corinthians 13:12, For now we are looking in a mirror that gives only a dim (blurred) reflection [of reality as in a riddle or enigma], but then [when perfection

comes] we shall see in reality and face to face! Now I know in part (imperfectly), but then I shall know and understand fully and clearly, even in the same manner as I have been fully and clearly known and understood [by God]. And so **Faith, Hope, Love** *[faith - conviction and belief respecting man's relation to God and divine things; hope - joyful and confident expectation of eternal salvation; love - true affection for God and man, growing out of God's love for and in us], these* **three**; *but the greatest of these is love.* Faith, Hope and Love are witnesses of a unified relationship with God. The Apostle Peter had a vision that details a voice answering from Heaven three times as a witness that what God has cleansed is no longer unclean. Peter, James and John witnessed Christ's transfiguration. Three witnesses in the book of Revelation...

~Word Of The Lord~

Peter heard the cock crow three times, confirming what Christ had foretold. Mary remained with Elizabeth for three months. A multitude waited with Christ three days without food. After three days, Jesus was found sitting in the Temple among the elders.

The heavenly hosts were divided into thirds: the Messenger Angels, the Warrior Angels, and the Worship Angels led by Michael, Gabriel and Lucifer. God used the number three to execute correction, protection, instruction, consecration, and confirmation of His Word. There were three items in the Ark of the Covenant. It is apparent, God finds identity and comfort in the number three. Strong's Concordance defines the word ***three*** in the Hebrew as an ***instrument of music, triangle, three stringed lute, a general of the third rank (the highest), captain, lord, a great measure, and prince.***

~*The Circle Of Agreement*~

Colossians 1:20, And God purposed that through (by the service, the intervention of) Him [the Son] all things should be completely reconciled back to Himself, whether on earth or in heaven, as through Him, [the Father] made peace by means of the blood of His cross.

God had a plan, through the intervention of Christ, everything would be reconciled back to Himself whether in Heaven or on earth by the Blood of the Cross. He created a perfect Circle of Agreement through Christ, His Blood and Agreement. This was the original covenant agreement.

The Circle of Agreement between the Father, the Son, and the Holy Spirit is the never-ending, perpetual cycle of what is, what was, and what is to come.

Anything born of God has had its conception through the Circle of Agreement and must be birthed, sustained, and completed by God. Everything we do as people of God must:

...begin in agreement.
...exist in agreement.
...have its completion in agreement.

That is the Circle of Agreement. ***It is the perpetuity of three.***

Two creates a linear movement which is the Law of Reciprocity. Three creates a circular movement which is the Law of Agreement. ***What was, what is, and what is to come.***

Hebrews 12:2a, Looking away [from all that will distract] to Jesus, Who is the Leader and the Source of our faith [giving the first incentive for our belief] and is also its Finisher [bringing it to maturity and perfection].

This is the full circle of anything that exists in God. Sadly, the Church has wrongly positioned itself in self-existence. It has failed to recognize the law of agreement. The Church functions on the principle of reciprocity and not creative faith; *I give to you, you give to me.* There is no "newness" in reciprocity.

When the disciples informed Jesus that His *natural* family was looking for Him, He responded by saying, *"My family are those who do the will of My Father."* Jesus placed a greater importance on His association with people, who were about His Father's business, than with His own biological family.

A person does not qualify as agreeing if the only people he agrees with are his own blood relatives. Many of the marriages I have counseled, in my tenure as a pastor, have had their greatest problem with the inability to separate from their biological families. They support their position with the philosophy, "Blood is thicker than water." This is the whole premise behind the passage, "A man shall leave his mother and a woman leave her home…" Agreement with your spouse takes precedence over all other relationships.

Covenant is imperative for producing godly offspring (Malachi 2). Reciprocity can only produce of its own kind. The moment a third entity is added, the result is something never before seen. This is where the favor of agreement is produced. There must be a third entity for newness. Agreement is so much more than just the exchange of suitable jargon; it is the adhesive that fastens and holds the many different parts of the Body of Christ together.

The Body of Christ is held together solely by the Power of Agreement. *Ephesians 4:16, For because of Him the whole body (the Church, in all its various parts), closely joined and firmly knit together by the joints and ligaments with which it is supplied, when each part [with power adapted to its need] is working properly [in all its functions], grows to full maturity, building itself up in love.*Within the organization of the Church, there is as much diversity as there are varieties of fish in the sea:

…we are not of the same race.

…we are not the same color.

…we come from different socio-economic levels.

The only thing the Church has in common, in the natural, is being a part of the human race. Agreement provides a cohesiveness that unites the Church as one body. *I Peter 2:10 (KJV), Which in time past were not a people, but are now the people of God; which had not obtained mercy but now have obtained mercy.* As my precious friends, Reba and Dony McGuire, so aptly penned in one of their songs:

We are that people who were not;

God's peculiar people who were not.
The seed of Abraham, the sons of God
A chosen generation,
A witness for all the world to see.
We are that people, we are,
We're the people of God.
We're not Black or White, No!
We're not bond nor free.
We're no earthly race.
We're a brand new breed.
We are that people, we are,
We're the people of God.

How can the Church continue to walk in the obscurity of spiritual blindness, thinking the dismemberment of the Body of Christ can be overlooked? We are to be a Body fitly joined together, where every joint supplies, adding to the whole. How does one overlook the undertones of jealousy, envy, and strife among pastors and associate pastors?

...among church members?

...among husbands and wives?

...among church denominations?

There are people who work together in Sunday Schools and touch the lives of children, then uproot, divorcing themselves from the church. What do you suppose this kind of behavior does to a child? If you have survived a divorce, you know the emotional and sometimes irreversible damages that children must endure.

Without the adhesive of agreement…
Without the discipline of faithfulness…

The Church is doomed. It is fragmented and divided. *John 17:21-23, That they all may be **one**, [just] as You, Father, are in Me and I in You, that they also may be **one** in us, so that the world may believe and be convinced that You have sent Me. I have given to them the glory and honor which You have given me, that they may be **one** [even] as We are **One**: I in them and You in me, in order that they may become **one** and perfectly united, that the world may know and [definitely] recognize that You sent me and that You have loved them [even] as You have loved me.*

Of the countless agreements God made with man, the third account is God's agreement with Abraham. *Genesis 15:18, On the same day the Lord made a covenant (promise, pledge) with Abram, saying, To your descendants I have given this land, from the river Egypt to the great river Euphrates…* God's covenant with Abraham was all about seeds, multiplicity of descendants and land. The prosperity of future generations was contingent upon Abraham's ability to carry out the demands of his agreement.

If the blessings found in Deuteronomy 28, were contingent upon you remaining in the agreement, where would the Church be today? Would you be able to find the agreeable factor and thus, become the intermediary of posterity like Abraham? Would your offspring be an Isaac or an Ishmael? The Book of Genesis records Abraham's willingness to remain in the agreement that established the covenant of blessings between God and all future generations.

Abraham became the father of many nations as was detailed in his agreement. His obedience to the covenant became the reward and linkage to prosperity. **By one man's obedience, God's everlasting covenant of blessings became the heritage of the servants of the Lord.** *Genesis 17:13b, My covenant shall be in your flesh for an everlasting covenant.*

John, the Revelator, closes out the scene in Revelation with an account of the thousands that will sing to the Lamb: the nations, kindred and tongues, the elders, the angels, and the beasts. Everything will come full circle and ultimately, God will be worshipped. *"And they sang, Holy, holy, holy, Lord God Almighty, which was, and is, and is to come."*

PRAYER OF AGREEMENT:

Father, I celebrate the Oneness of the Godhead. Bring my spirit into unity and agreement with Your Holy Spirit. I offer up my body, soul and spirit, make me one as I worship You.

Amen

POWER KEY:

~Agreement Is The Foundation Of All Existence.

~11~

THE FRUIT OF AGREEMENT

Power Key: *The Fruit Of Agreement Is Favor.*

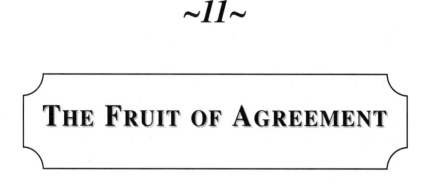 here are two different types of Favor available to you. The Favor of man and the Favor of God and are both unlocked through agreement. One produces "things" and one produces the "glory of God."

The more agreeable you are, the more Favor you will reap. *Proverbs 12:2 (KJV), A good man obtaineth favour of the Lord.* The Favor of man is contingent upon your willingness to *find the agreeable factor*. For example, when you dine at a restaurant and your server is having a bad day, the more agreeable you are; the more favorable your service will be. Regardless of his or her trials, your agreeable spirit unlocks Favor! If you will purpose to find something agreeable in every situation with every person you attend to, you will unlock Favor every time. Favor will supply you with money when money cannot buy you Favor. Favor can take you further than your talents, gifts or skills. If you will just become agreeable, a rich man could pay your way around the world. Disagreeable people do not go very far.

The number one car salesman in the nation, whose record breaking sales are recorded in the Guinness Book of World Records, uses the strategy of finding the agreeable factor. When a customer approaches with their trade-in vehicle, he compliments their choice of color or the amount of miles they have been able to utilize. He discovered the agreeable factor was the defining link between his customer's satisfaction and his pocket book.

~*Four Factors To Facilitate Favor*~

~*1st Factor - Agreement*~

Agreement is obviously at the top of the list in facilitating Favor. The more agreeable, the more humble you are, the more favored you become. The Bible says, *"God will give grace, favor and blessing to the humble..."* Agreeable people generate Favor. My father was a very favored person. He had well over a thousand people show up at his funeral when he passed away. He was not a believer until his latter days, yet, he had the ability to unlock Favor. People were easily drawn to him. Despite all his faults and unhealthy habits, he was a kindhearted man. It was his ability to find something to connect with that caused people to Favor him. The Favor of man is unlocked without the need to access faith.

~2nd Factor - Appearance~

There is no mystery to the statistic that states 98% of all people hired are hired based on their appearance. You have probably seen the advertisement that reads: "Image is Everything." You are a walking billboard. *Esther 5:2,3, And when the king saw Esther the queen standing in the court, **she obtained favor** in his sight, and he held out to [her] the golden scepter that was in his hand. So Esther drew near and touched the tip of the scepter. Then the king said to her, What will you have, Queen Esther? **What is your request? It shall be given you,** even to the half of the kingdom.* Esther's appearance became her pathway to obtaining favor with the king of Persia. It was a known custom and decree that no one could approach the king without his summons, and the penalty was death. Esther risked her life to save her people, and her detailed attention to self care was her key to uncommon favor. The Bible records that the king extended his golden scepter toward her. That sounds like Favor to me! People see what you are before they hear what you say. Image is everything!

~3rd Factor - Kindness~

Power Key: *One Act Of Kindness Can Link You To A Lifetime Of Favor.*

*Psalm 30:5a, For His anger is but for a moment, but His **favor** is for a lifetime or in His **favor** is life.* Rahab the harlot obtained Favor because of her kindness.

Her one act of kindness paved the way for justification as is recorded in the Book of James 2:15. The writer states: *"So also with Rahab the harlot - was she not shown to be justified (pronounced righteous before God) by [good] deeds when she took in the scouts (spies) and sent them away by a different route?"* She agreed to show kindness to the messengers of God and she obtained righteousness. In other words, she secured a pardon for her evil life-style. That is Favor! *Proverbs 3:34, Though He scoffs at the scoffers and scorns the scorners, yet He gives His undeserved favor to the low [in rank], the humble, and the afflicted.* It does not matter how low you are on the totem-pole; you can obtain the Favor of God.

~4th Factor - Problem Solving~

Joseph was a problem solver, he obtained Favor when he first entered Potiphar's house because he was a model slave. His excellence in servanthood caused him to be noticed by Potiphar. He later was imprisoned for a crime he did not commit, and still, he provided solutions for those around him. His ability and willingness to interpret the dreams of his fellow inmates paved a way of Favor right out of jail into the position of second in command. Your ability to solve a problem, wherever you may be today, is your key to Favor. *Genesis 41:41-43, Then Pharaoh said to Joseph, See, I have set you over all the land of Egypt. And Pharaoh took of his [signet] ring from his hand and put it on Joseph's hand, and arrayed him in [official] vestments of fine linen and put a gold chain about his neck; He made him to ride in the second*

chariot which he had, and [officials] cried before him, Bow the knee! And he set him over all the land of Egypt. Solving the right problem will produce promotion every time.

In the conclusion of Jacob's life, he pronounces a blessing upon his sons. Joseph's favorable disposition and willingness to forgive and remain in agreement with his brothers, despite their evil intentions, afforded him not only the **Favor of man**, but the **Favor of God**. The blessing spoken over Joseph was multiplied and was greater than that of Abraham's, Isaac's and Jacob's combined. The Bible says, *"...blessings lying in the deep beneath, blessings of the breasts of the womb. ...and are as lasting as the bounties of the eternal hills; they shall be on the head of Joseph, and on the crown of the head of him who was the consecrated one and the one separated from his brethren and [the one who] is prince among them."* Anyone may facilitate favor through any of the four factors mentioned, but only those who remain free from offense can unlock the favor of God.

~The Favor Of God~

Within the glory of God, is a realm of blessings that cannot be accessed through any other realm but agreement. *Romans 2:10-11, But **glory** and **honor** and [heart] **peace** shall be awarded to everyone who [habitually] does good, the Jew first and also the Greek (Gentile). For God shows no partiality [undue favor or unfairness; with Him, one man is not different from another].* Do not misinterpret the latter part of this passage which says, "For God shows no partiality…" This is not implying that He will not show *Favor*; rather, it is saying that He will not show *"undue Favor."* The word *partiality* or *respect,* as stated in the King James Version in the Greek, means favoritism, acceptor of a face, countenance, and appearance. The Favor of God will be seen upon your face, your countenance and your appearance. The prerequisite for Favor, as found in this passage, is *"habitually does good."* The word *good* comes from the two Greek words meaning, benefit, valuable, virtuous, beautiful, worthy, honest, abide, *agree,* lighten the ship and *band together*. In other words, the person who stays habitually in agreement will be awarded **GLORY**, **HONOR** and **PEACE**. *Within these three words is hidden the Favor of God.*

As I began to research the topic of the Favor of God, I stumbled across Romans 2:10,11. In essence, it is saying God has no favorites. I was having a difficult time accepting this, since I have always declared myself as God's favorite. I must say the blessings that have come upon my life are truly proof of some kind of reward system beyond the scope of my faith. It is more than the Favor of man.

Power Key: *Worship Releases The Favor Of God.*

Finding the agreeable factor and applying it unlocks the Favor of man; worship filled with gratitude releases the Favor of God.

Power Key: *Gratitude Unlocks The Mercy Of God And The Mercy Of God Unlocks The Favor Of God.*

In Psalm 136, known for the repetition of the "mercy of the Lord", the word **mercy** comes from the Hebrew word *cheçed* meaning *kindness, piety; beauty, favor, good deed.*

The word **glory**, in the Greek, is *doxa* which is the root word for doxology, meaning worship. The favor of God is not released, except you remain in agreement and offer up true worship.

The word **honor**, in the Greek means value, money paid, dignity, price, *and the highest degree of esteem.* This sounds like favor to me. In addition, this is your reward for staying in agreement and offering up true worship!

The word **peace**, means *to join, prosperity, and quietness, set at one again.* Here is the fruit of Favor once again! You are promised prosperity accompanied by peace.

Favor is more than just going around proclaiming the acceptable year of the Lord. It is much deeper than claiming a parking space in the front row at the grocery store; it is about the glory of God! It is about pardon! *Proverbs 3:3,4, Let not mercy and kindness [shutting out all hatred and selfishness] and truth [shutting out all deliberate hypocrisy or falsehood] forsake you; bind them about your neck, write them upon the tablet of your heart. So shall you find favor, good understanding, and high esteem in the sight [or judgment] of God and man.* Again, the word mercy comes from the Hebrew word *cheçed* meaning **Favor.**

The word Favor as used in the opening text of Proverbs 12:2, derives its meaning from the Hebrew words *râtsôwn & râtsâh* meaning, delight, desire, good pleasure, satisfy, approve, and *pardon.*

The Favor of God is like receiving a pardon for all your past mistakes. While God forgives sin, it is a completely different situation to receive a pardon. A pardon is like a letter that exonerates every mistake, even beyond those forgiven.

*Deuteronomy 8:18b, For it is He who gives you power to get wealth, that He may establish His covenant (agreement)...*There is a level of blessings available to the believer that goes beyond the increase of sowing and reaping, into the wealth of God. I shared with you in Chapter 8 – *Agreement and Worship* – the third level of warring in the Spirit is acquiring Wealth and Riches through worship.

It is absurd for Christians to sit around waiting for some millionaire to pass on in hopes of becoming the recipient of his wealth. Yet, entire congregations are locked into this mentality of prosperity. I firmly believe that God will not entrust the wealth of some diligent, hard working heathen into the hands of some lazy Christian. Why would He transfer the wealth of the wicked into the hands of poor stewards? The wealth of the believer is enveloped in the agreement. (More on this topic in Chapter 12)

Power Key: *You Have The Power To Perpetuate Anything You Want Through The Power Of The Seed.*

Seedtime and harvest are one aspect of God's plan for provision. When you embrace the truth of God's Word as directed by the Apostle Paul in *II Corinthians 9:6 (KJV), But this I say, He which soweth sparingly shall reap also sparingly; and he which soweth bountifully shall reap also bountifully.* You receive remuneration based on the 30, 60, 100-fold return. The blessings of seed-faith sowing are contingent upon the basic laws of prosperity.

Jeremiah 29:11, For I know the thoughts and plans that I have for you, says the Lord, thoughts and plans for welfare and peace and not for evil, to give you hope in your final outcome. Within the matrix of God's blessings, there is a reward system that produces wealth. This is the Favor of God.

A matrix is the veinstone where a precious metal takes form until it is discovered. I believe there is a matrix, a womb of covenant blessings in God, which the Church has not yet recognized.

Offense causes the believer to respond imperviously to the plan, robbing them of the wealth as promised in Deuteronomy 28. This compensation plan works only in conjunction with agreement.

The seed sown in faith produces what you want while the seed wrapped in agreement produces what God wants for you. The difference: *what you want for yourself is based on what you can visualize, what God wants for you is limitless, immeasurable, and boundless.*

Power Key: *The Seed Sown on the Wings of Worship Unlocks the Unimaginable.*

Ephesians 3:20, Now to Him who, by (in conse-quence of) the [action of His] power that is at work with-in us, is able to [carry out His purpose and] do super-abundantly, far over and above all that we [dare] ask or think [infinitely beyond our highest prayers, desires, thoughts, hopes, or dreams] —

There are things which have never even entered your mind that God wants to do for you! It is what I call the **Reward System** of God. It is based on the integrity of your heart. Worship becomes the transporter for your seed which elevates it to a higher dimension and causes it to yield a higher increase.

Matthew 5:12, Be glad and supremely joyful, for your reward in heaven is great (strong and intense), for in this same way people persecuted the prophets who were before you. Your rewards have already been estab-lished in Heaven. They cannot exist in this realm until you have aligned yourself with the Holy Spirit. Jesus taught the disciples how to have a little Heaven on earth. He said, "Thy kingdom come, Thy will be done, on earth as it is in Heaven." The rewards of Heaven are available to you now! When we all get to Heaven and stand before the throne of God, rewards will have little or no value. What would be the purpose of rewards when we behold the Lamb?

Matthew 16:27,28 (KJV) says, *For the Son of man shall come in the glory of His Father with his angels; and then He shall **reward** every man according to his works. Verily I say unto you, There be some standing here, which shall not taste of death, till they see the Son of man com-ing in his kingdom.* This passage guarantees rewards for the believer based on works when Jesus comes into the glory of His Father.

    Matthew 17:1-8, And six days after this, Jesus took with Him Peter and James and John his brother, and led them up on a high mountain by themselves. And His appearance underwent a change in their presence; and His face shone clear and bright like the sun, and His clothing became as white as light. And behold, there appeared to them Moses and Elijah, who kept talking with Him. Then Peter began to speak and said, to Jesus, Lord, it is good and delightful that we are here; if you approve, I will put up three booths here – One for You and one for Moses and one for Elijah. While he was still speaking, behold, a shining cloud [composed of light] overshadowed them, and a voice from the cloud said, This is My Son, My Beloved, with Whom I am [and have always been] delighted. Listen to Him! When the disciples heard it, they fell on their faces and were seized with alarm and struck with fear. But Jesus came and touched them and said, Get up, and do not be afraid. And when they raised their eyes, they saw no one but Jesus only. Jesus experienced the glory of the Father and was brought into His kingdom. This transfiguration activated the reward system of God. You do not have to wait a lifetime before accessing your rewards.

    Christians do not understand the principles of God's reward system, because they are conditioned by the rudimentary teachings of sowing and reaping. *A reward is like receiving a surprise from glory.* They are unscheduled, uncommon gifts from the warehouse of Heaven. God is a God of "suddenlies". He thrills at the sight of His children as the Holy Spirit – the Revealer, unwraps His gifts making them visible. *James 1:17, Every good gift and every perfect (free, large, full) gift is from above; it comes down from the Father of all [that gives] light, in [the shining of] Whom there can be no variation [rising or setting] or shadow cast by His turning [as in an eclipse].*

The rewards of Heaven are perfect and eternal unlike the corruptible rewards of man. Break free from the tradition of expecting only a harvest and search with anticipation for the rewards that are out of this world! *Matthew 6:20 (KJV), But lay up for yourselves treasures in heaven, where neither moth nor rust doth corrupt, and where thieves do not break through nor steal: for where your treasure is, there will your heart be also.* The seed mingled with worship is like a direct deposit into your heavenly account.

Power Key: *The Fragrance Of Agreement Is Worship.*

Worship is the only gift man gives to God that ascends beyond the principalities in high places directly into His throne room. It is like a fragrance that creates a sweet smelling savor to His nostrils. Launch your seed on the wings of worship and store for yourself treasures in Heaven. God makes deposits into your account on the premise of your obedience and your faith. *Romans 4:5, Abraham believed in God (trusted in) God, and it was credited to his account as righteousness (right living and right standing with God).*

The seed of agreement is much like someone

depositing a measure of funds into an account that yields a much higher interest. It can be compared to a certificate of deposit which requires no maintenance or effort on the part of its investor. It is left alone until it reaches maturity.

When you sow a seed into the life of a man or woman of God whose anointing you respect, you enter into an agreement that qualifies you to join the commonwealth of God's elect. Your seeds make their way into the womb of the supernatural where everything has its origin.

Romans 4:17b (KJV), ...before Him whom He believed, even God, who quickeneth the dead, and calleth those things, which be not as though they were.

Power Key: ***Every Seed Sown Yields A Harvest.***

The Bible instructs the believer to walk by faith and not by sight. *II Corinthians 5:7, For we **walk** by faith, not by sight,* Every time you sow a seed, you will reap a harvest. ***Faith is not a requirement for sowing the seed.*** The seed principles work for the just and the unjust alike. These are the fundamentals of sowing and reaping. You may be asking yourself, what about Mark 11:24? The entire Word of Faith prosperity movement is hinged on the principle: *"Therefore I say unto you, What things soever ye desire, when ye pray, believe that ye receive them, and ye shall have them."*

Prosperity is not dependent upon faith; ***it is the expected effect of the laws of sowing and reaping.*** One papaya seed produces several hundred papaya plants yielding an increase of seeds too numerous to tell. This is the law of cause and effect.

So, then, what is faith? According to Hebrews 11:6, it is belief in God that He exists and that He is a Rewarder of them that diligently seek Him. The purpose of faith is for pleasing God and obtaining a good report as did the elders of our faith. *Hebrews 11:1-3 (KJV), Now faith is the substance of things hoped for, the evidence of things not seen. For by it the elders obtained a good report. Through faith we understand that the worlds were framed by the Word of God, so that things which are seen were not made of things which do appear.* The "things hoped for" is not referring to the things which are visible. The hope is for "Christ in you the hope of glory". You do not hope for a car; you sow for a car. You do not hope for a house; you sow for a house.

Faith, then, is being at the right place at the right time when the Holy Ghost unveils things from the supernatural. Remember, everything you want already exists in the realm of the unseen. Begin calling those things which be not as though they were, *because they are!* If things did not exist in the supernatural, God would not direct you to call them forth.

Allow me to use the Master Key of Agreement to unlock a revelation of blessings unlike you may have never experienced. I was ministering at Dr. Murdock's Wisdom Conference in December, 1999. I sowed a seed of $1,000.00; it is not unusual for me to sow a seed of this level. Although I did not have a specific need at that time, I gave nonetheless. My giving was based on the respect I have for Mike Murdock and his ministry. In essence, I released my seed into the hands of agreement. Unsure of its potential, I placed my confidence in God's reward system. *Hebrews 10:35,36 (KJV), Cast not away therefore your confidence, which hath great recompense of reward. For ye have need of patience, that, after ye have done the will of God, ye might receive the promise.* It was my covenant relationship with Dr. Murdock that prompted me to sow the seed.

Power Key: ***The Seed Of Agreement Receives Its Assignment From God.***

Matthew 7:11 (KJV), If ye then, being evil, know how to give good gifts unto your children, how much more shall your Father which is in heaven give good things to them that ask him? I remember Dr. Murdock asking us to repeat the statement, "I'm not coming out of the agreement." Instead of asking for "things" in return, I sowed the seed in agreement and transported it on the wings of my worship.

I believe the only petitions that make it to the warehouse of Heaven are those offered with an attitude of worship. ***Worship is the character of one's heart; it questions the motive of expectation.*** Could it be possible, if I had placed an assignment on my seed as I am accustomed to doing, it would have been out of greed, since I had no real need? Never mingle your greed with your seed. This level of wealth can only be unlocked through agreement. When I purposed to come into agreement with Dr. Murdock, I had no idea the increase would exceed my wildest imagination. Within a matter of weeks, God moved on the hearts of many to sow $1,000.00 dollar gifts into my life. I have received, on the average, a $1,000.00 dollar harvest every 3 to 4 days. I have just opened today's mail and guess what was in it? You guessed it, another check for $1,000.00! The seed sown, with no specific expectation of return, has yielded an unexpected harvest! Do not misunderstand what I just said. This level of sowing has an anticipated response from God as opposed to expecting what one can conceive. Dr. Murdock's paraphrase of Ephesians 6:8 says, *"What you make happen for others, God will make happen for you."* That takes the expectation off your seed and allows God to give the assignment. This is a completely new level of expectation. **Expecting the unexpected!**

Power Key: *Worship Is The Seed Of Intimacy That Conceives The Unimaginable.*

I believe my willingness to enter into covenant agreement with a man of God unlocked a supernatural well of abundance in my life. It has been an incredible year!

Deuteronomy 8:18, But you shall [earnestly] remember the Lord your God, for it is He Who gives you power to get wealth, that He may establish His covenant which He swore to your fathers, as it is this day. God is willing to lead you into wealth based on His *(covenant) agreement* with your forefathers, Abraham, Isaac and Jacob. He is bound to His Word; can He count on your word? God can never breach His agreement. *You are the*

only one who can abort the promise of agreement.

Your willingness to embrace this truth, on the reward system of God, is the deciding factor whether or not it will work for you. *II Chronicles 20:20 (KJV), Believe on the Lord so shall ye be established, believe in His prophets so shall ye prosper.*

Power Key: *Agreement With The Man Of God Is More Valuable Than Your Harvest, Because He Is Your Connection To Wealth.*

You may be able to speak in tongues, prophesy, and still, wonder how you are going to keep food on your table. Your problem does not originate from a lack of prayer and intercession. Instead, it is your inability to recognize a man of God. *Hosea 4:9, My people perish for a lack of [recognition] knowledge.* The problem is not a faith problem; it is your lack of recognition of one who can deliver you.

~You may reject a teacher and miss good teaching.
~You may reject an evangelist and lose some motivation.
~You may reject an apostle and miss order in your life.
~You may reject a pastor and lose your covering.
~When you reject a prophet, you reject your hope for the future.

Thus saith the Lord, Do not reject this word You are on the brink of moving to the level of the unimaginable. This chapter may be challenging your mindsets about sowing and reaping. Do not allow those teachings to become a "sacred golden cow" in your life. Topple

those cows and agree with God's Word for your life right now!

PRAYER OF AGREEMENT:

Heavenly Father, I thank You for Your Favor in my life. Thank You for the pardon that Your mercy affords me. I wrap my seeds with agreement and ask that You produce what You want for me. You know me better than I know myself. I lift up my seed on the wings of my worship.

Amen

POWER KEYS:

~The Fruit Of Agreement Is Favor.
~One Act Of Kindness Can Link You To A Lifetime Of Favor.
~Worship Releases The Favor Of God.
~Gratitude Unlocks The Mercy Of God And The Mercy Of God Unlocks The Favor Of God.
~You Have The Power To Perpetuate Anything You Want Through The Power Of The Seed.
~The Seed Sown On The Wings Of Worship Unlocks The Unimaginable.
~The Fragrance Of Agreement Is Worship.
~Every Seed Sown Yields A Harvest.
~The Seed Of Agreement Receives Its Assignment From God.
~Worship Is The Seed Of Intimacy That Conceives The Unimaginable.
~Agreement With The Man Of God Is More Valuable Than Your Harvest, Because He Is Your Connection To Wealth.

~12~

The Wealth of Agreement

Power Key: *The Power Of Wealth Is The Means Of Influence To The World.*

The Bible says, in the Book of Ecclesiastes, money is the answer for everything. Money is paradoxical; it is man's answer for everything and yet, the corruptor of many good men. It is the very thing that pits brother against brother, husband against wife. It has been the demise of great nations and empires. Money has become the antithesis of the moral fiber of our country. No longer are character, integrity and truth at the forefront of morality. Instead, people listen for the sound that has been ringing since Judas accepted the thirty pieces of silver in exchange for the betrayal of Christ. Thus, money has become the major influence and voice of the world. The Church can no longer run from the responsibility of creating wealth for the purpose of changing our world. When the Church understands this power, it will then become the strong voice of moral influence God intended from the beginning.

In Chapter Eleven, I discussed the seed that carries an anticipated response from God as opposed to the expectation of what you can conceive. I sowed a seed into a man of God, and activated its harvest through the Power of Agreement. Agreement then, has a power unto itself. Agreement has a spirit – the Holy Spirit.

Power Key: *Agreement Is The Most Powerful Force In The Universe By Its Very Nature.*

God wants to use the wealth, described in Deuteronomy 8:18, to show the world the proof of His agreement with His people. Yet, Christians passively sit in front of their television sets hoping to hear a "word from the Lord" that will deliver them from the struggles of daily grind.

The Bible is filled with Scripture describing the kind of victorious life the believer should be living. *God is Agreement; He is creation looking for a place to happen.* He is like a tornado in search of a pathway to show forth His fearsome terror. God is ready. Are you?

Can you imagine what would happen if everyone in our local churches woke up Sunday morning with an agreeable attitude? Imagine the explosion of God's presence as each member of the Body of Christ moved in concerted effort with one another. If members took upon themselves the posture of humility, it would give way to an unstoppable move of faith. There would be no sickness. There would be no lack for love, no insufficiency, and doubt would virtually vanish. It is not enough to just talk about a move of the Spirit of this magnitude. The world is looking for firework displays to back up what the Church preaches.

In a world where science has uncovered so many deep, dark mysteries, there is a pressing need for a connecting link. The missing link is an agreeable factor; between a self-sufficient, sin-ridden society and a divided, self-glorified Church. When did the Church become so blinded and askewed to the virtues of unity and agreement? All the while, the world cries out with its hunger pangs for something/someone to provide satisfaction.

They yearn for a cohesiveness amidst their torn fragmented existence.

Power Key: *Wealth Is God's Reward For Agreement.*

Agreement is the healing agent for the imbalanced and maligned condition of the Body of Christ. Yet, we cannot offer healing to the world until we learn to heal ourselves.

Reaching out to a dying world is more than giving them a little bag of groceries at Thanksgiving and Christmas. The Church has lost its voice; not only in the White House, but also in the crack house, in the house where children are being abused, and in the house where the father is absent.

We have nothing to say, because we have no

power. I believe fully in the power of the Holy Spirit to set the captives free. I am fully persuaded this power was given for obtaining Wealth to reach a world that understands and finds its existence in money.

The Church must make the adjustment within itself and agree with the cultural paradigm shifts of society. The time has come for the saints to accumulate Wealth for being God's voice to the world. ***God gives you power to create Wealth and Wealth is power.*** What would be the benefit of belonging to an entity with no power and no voice?

There can be no changes in our culture until the law of agreement is factored into the equation of society's dismal future. History repeats itself and, with every passing, creates a pattern that can only be reformed through agreement.

Most Christians are looking for a "quick fix" from God. It would be nice if you could just sow a magical seed that would relieve everybody's pressures.

When the focus of the Church turns, from simply wanting to "feel" God to craving the wisdom of God, it will then begin to take on the likeness of its Creator.

Power Key: ***The Essence Of Wisdom Is Unlocked Through The Humility Of Worshipful Fear.***

Proverbs 1:7, The reverent and worshipful fear of the Lord is the beginning and principle and choice part of knowledge [its starting point and its essence].
Proverbs 4:7 (KJV) says, " Wisdom is the principle thing…"

Wisdom is unattainable outside of worship. Wisdom begins when you have humbly acquiesced to the will of God through your worship. Its origin is found in your worshipful fear of the Word of God. It is a place in time when you finally agree. Despite all the erroneous teachings piled one on top of the other, it is that time when you choose His way and not your way. *Psalm 112:1-3, Praise the Lord (hallelujah!) blessed (Happy, fortunate, to be envied) is the man who fears (reveres and worships) the Lord, who delights greatly in His commandments. His (spiritual) offspring shall be mighty upon the earth; the generation of the upright. Prosperity and welfare are in his house, and his righteousness endures forever.*

This chapter would be incomplete without a stroll through Solomon's Court. He is known as the richest man who ever lived. God rewarded him with wisdom and riches, because he did not ask for them. His father started out as a shepherd boy and ended up a king. Still, Solomon's inherited royalty was not his celebrated difference. The connection to his father, the worshipper, was the key to his Wealth.

Power Key: *Worship Unlocks The Wealth Of God.*

The progression of Wealth is: first Agreement, second Worship, and third Wisdom.

- *There can be no worship without agreement.*
- *There can be no wisdom without worship.*

Before delving too deeply into the Wealth of King Solomon, allow me to share my views on the difference between Wealth and prosperity.

Wealth is what God gives those who seek His wisdom through worship. The avenue of worship creates an access to His presence and in His presence is fullness of joy. The desires of your heart are connected to your worship.

Power Key: *Desire Is Clothed In The Vesture Of Worship.*

When God's people delight themselves in His presence, He reciprocates by lavishing His love upon them. Worship creates an intimacy between the worshipper and the Father; it causes Him to react like a lover pursuing His beloved. God is in pursuit of worshippers.

Power Key: *Worship Incites God's Desire Toward Us.*

Each time you worship, God reaches into His treasure chest and adorns you with the jewels of companionship and covenant – the proof of His love. Worship is the combination that unlocks the vault of God's love, a calculated approach at romancing the heart of God:

> *...It is passionate pursuit.*
> *...Unconcealed eagerness.*
> *...A private display of affection.*

This intimate form of pursuing compels the Father to give you, *"everything your little heart desires."*

Ezekiel 16:10-14, I clothed you also with embroidered cloth and shod you with [fine seal] leather; and I girded you about with fine linen and covered you with silk. I decked you also with ornaments and I put bracelets on your wrists and a chain on your neck. And I put a ring on your nostril and earrings in your ears and a beautiful crown upon your head! Thus you were decked with gold and silver, and your raiment was of fine linen and silk and embroidered cloth; you ate fine flour and honey and oil. And you were exceedingly beautiful and you prospered into royal estate. And your renown went forth among the nations for your beauty, for it was perfect through my majesty and splendor which I have put upon you, says the Lord God. It is quite evident from the description Ezekiel gives that **Wealth is directly connected to your worship.** It is also evident that God is the One Who gives the power [ability] to get Wealth.

Flip the golden coin of God's plan for provision and look into the structure of prosperity with me. Prosperity is based on God's principles of increase. It is a result of the laws of sowing and reaping. To every principle in God's Word there is a natural "cause and effect" necessary for its fulfillment.

There is also an anointing that releases increase, but not based on earthly principles; instead, it is based on spiritual principles. As God's people, the Church has been afforded the privilege of reaping the increase of the natural and spirit realms as well.

~The Difference Between A Law And An Anointing~

There is a difference between a law or a principle and an anointing. I am quite certain that most believers have experienced the anointing of healing, prosperity, and possibly a prophetic anointing. A specific anointing will always break the yoke of its subject's bondage.

- A healing anointing destroys the yoke of bondage: disease.
- An anointing for finances destroys the yoke of bondage: debt.
- A prophetic anointing destroys the yoke of bondage: confusion.
- A worship anointing destroys the yoke of bondage: religion.

You may receive healing through prayer, but when you come into agreement with a "healing anointing," it not only brings healing, it also destroys the yoke of disease. It is vitally important to come into agreement with someone who has a "healing anointing" and not one with only faith to heal. There are psychics who have the power to heal; however, they have no anointing to destroy the bondage that caused the sickness.

When you apply "principles" of prosperity, you reap the "effect" of the laws of that principle. When you come under the Anointing of Agreement, you get what you sowed for and you also get what is released through the anointing.

Power Key: *The Anointing Of Agreement Breaks The Yoke Of Bondage Of Anything Agreed Upon.*

Agreement is like a street...

A golden street...

It is filled with blessings, Wealth, favor, surprises and the unimaginable. Proverbs refers to the road of wisdom as a highway of pleasantness and paths of peace. To enjoy these blessings, you must stay on the road and obey the signals. *Psalm 37:23 (KJV), The steps of a good man are ordered by the Lord: and he delighteth in his way.*

~Agreement Positions You For Victory Every Time~

You will never lose when you choose the avenue of agreement. *It puts you at the right place, at the right time, every time.*

You have already been positioned to operate in Favor by virtue of your agreement to read this book. Begin sowing the seed of agreement immediately. I mentioned earlier *every seed sown has a harvest.* That is a law. Law requires no faith. When a seed of hate is sown, it yields a harvest of mistrust and judgment. When seeds of jealousy and envy are sown, there is a harvest of strife and evil. You do not need faith to see the harvest of these seeds. Naturally, you do not want to expend your faith for a return on bad seed sown. Therefore, the law of sowing and reaping is available to God's people for increase, but it is not His supernatural provision for Wealth.

God calls Himself Jehovah Jireh which means *"God's provision shall be seen."* He is declaring Himself... He is obligating Himself... to be your provider! God is going to make provision for you, regardless of your seed, based on the covenant He made with Abraham, Isaac and Jacob.

My children are not required to sow seeds to reap "provision" in our home. Their needs are met according to my "riches" in my bank account. If they want to reap something extraordinary, they must sow seeds of obedience: they may clean their rooms, help their mother with the dishes, or take out the trash. I can reward them for the seeds of obedience, but they must remain in my home. *Philippians 4:19, And my God will liberally supply "fill to the full" your every need according to His riches in glory in Christ Jesus.*

The Scripture says, *"...according to His riches in glory in Christ Jesus."* He will supply your needs according to the warehouse of Heaven if you are **"in agreement" (in Christ Jesus).** It was through Christ's blood that a new agreement (covenant) was drawn up. Therefore, God can only supply your needs if you remain in (covenant) agreement through Christ.

~Sowing In Desperation~

The motive behind many believers' sowing is desperation. Their choices and decisions have brought them to a place where they must sow seed to survive. Somewhere along the way, they cut off their provision. The Covenant God, Jehovah-Jireh, was restricted from supplying their needs. Then, they are forced to live off their seed, instead of relying on "The Provider".

God never intended for His covenant people to be maintained by their seeds. The tithe, as mentioned in

Malachi 3:11, is for rebuking the devourer. It is meant for provision. Seed sowing is an available source for increase, but not for provision. Dr. Murdock says, God will never give you anything that can replace His presence. He tells a story of ministering at a church where they kept back half of the offerings received for his ministry. He refused to accept any part of the offering, recognizing his Provider as Jehovah-Jireh. He knew his provision was not in the harvest of the seed he sowed into that church.

If you rely on sowing the seed for your provision, you have cut God out of the equation. The principles of sowing and reaping work for the godly and the ungodly alike. *Matthew 5:45 (KJV), That ye may be the children of your father which is in heaven; for he maketh his sun to rise on the evil and on the good, and sendeth rain on the just and on the unjust.* When you look to God as your Jehovah-Jireh (your Provider), you are never confined to the hope of faith in a seed, but rather to the assurance of His power, provision and prosperity.

Power Key: *Wealth Is The Product Of Yielding To A Higher Level Of Increase.*

The world's system is based on compensation for services rendered. It is what is known as a free enterprise system. In this system, ***anyone*** may participate. The world is living off the principles of sowing and reaping. Hence, when disaster strikes, they have no hope of provision.

Am I saying sowing and reaping is wrong or that it

is of no consequential value? A big, emphatic no! I am saying, the Body of Christ should be sowing not out of necessity, but out of joy. The Bible clearly states, *"God loves a cheerful giver."* A sower should always be happy to sow seed, knowing that his provision is not coming from the harvest of that seed. His provision comes from God.

A seed should never be sown for a new car or a new house. A seed is sown to acquire Wealth to carry out God's work. Paul wrote in the Book of Phillipians, *"And my God will liberally supply (fill to the full) your every **need** according to His riches in glory in Christ Jesus."* The problem here is most Christians are not walking "in Christ Jesus". They are out of fellowship, out of agreement, operating in offense, and then they place their hope on a seed praying it yields a harvest to meet their needs. A house and a car are needs. These things will be met according to God's riches in glory by Christ Jesus.

When a believer is in good standing with the Lord faithfully paying his tithes, he is already promised the blessings of Abraham according to Deuteronomy 28. This is based on obedience to the ordinances of God's Word.

~Three Areas Of Blessings Available To The Believer~

~Jehovah-Jireh is your Provider – Condition: Tithing.
~Favor unlocks the unexpected – Condition: Agreement.
~The Wealth of God – Condition: Sowing and Reaping.

Phillipians 4:18, But I have [your full payment]

*and more; I have everything I need and am amply sup-
plied, now that I have received from Epaphroditus the
gifts you sent me. [They are the] fragrant odor of an
offering and sacrifice which God welcomes and in which
He delights.* The Apostle Paul was in a partnership with
the church of Philippi and **all of his needs were met and
then some.** The people's offerings were received as a fragrant act of worship in which God delights. These were
seeds of worship that unlock the wealth of God for the
perpetuity of the gospel.

Power Key: ***Where There Is Agreement There Is
Abundance.***

God continually places man in positions where he
must cry out to Him. God will keep you in situations
where you must believe Him. He does not want you to
place your hope and trust in a seed. The Book of
Proverbs directs the reader to lean on, trust in, and be
confident in the Lord. It calls for honoring the Lord with
the first part of all your income. This is referring to paying the tithe not sowing. Tithing is an ordinance that
complies with God's Word. Obedience to this ordinance
promises that your storage places will be filled and your
vats will be overflowing with new wine. This refers to an
abundance in provision. The Psalmist also wrote, *"I've
never seen the righteous forsaken, nor his seed begging
for bread."* This is a level of provision where you have
all you need. You lack for nothing. *The Lord is my
Shepherd; I shall not want for any good thing...*
As we read earlier, in Hebrews 11:6, *Without faith*

it is impossible to please Him: for he that cometh to God must believe that He is, and that He is a rewarder of them that diligently seek Him. This has no reference to diligently seeking seeds to meet your needs. It is instructing you to place your trust in His provision of promise.

What happens when a person is completely dependent on what they sow, instead of abiding in the provision of Jehovah-Jireh? This is when a provider is desperately needed. The Bible says, in *Genesis 26:12 (KJV), Then Isaac sowed in that land and received in the same year an hundred fold: and the Lord blessed him.* Isaac was in the middle of a famine. The conditions that surrounded Isaac's ability to sow and reap were very poor. Yet, the Bible says, he sowed in the time of famine and, within the same year, reaped a one hundred-fold harvest. Where do you suppose Isaac (a son of the Covenant Agreement) got water for his seed? From God – Jehovah Jireh.

As I mentioned earlier, my children do not have to live off their seeds; they are sustained by my provision. Their obedience and good deeds unlock my favor for whatever their heart desires. Remember the Scripture, *Delight yourself in the Lord and He shall give thee the desires of thine heart?* Albeit, my children could grow up, reject and rebel against the standard of conduct in our home and choose to leave. They have, now, cut off their supply and are forced to live off what they can supply. They have come out of the agreement.

When you break the covenant of God through offense, you are cutting off your part of the inheritance in the agreement. *II Corinthians 9:7, Let each one [give] as*

he has made up his own mind and purposed in his heart, not reluctantly or sorrowfully or under compulsion, for God loves (He takes pleasure in, prizes above other things, and is unwilling to abandon or to do without) a cheerful (joyous, "prompt to do it") giver [whose heart is in his giving].

This clearly states, the condition for sowing a seed is when you have no need. Verse 8 says, *So that you may always and under all circumstances and whatever the need be self-sufficient [possessing enough to require no aid or support and furnished in abundance for every good work and charitable donation].*

When you sow seed based on your willingness to agree, you reap a blessing *...done of our Father, who is in heaven.* When God does something, He always does it in grand style; because that is the way He is. *Galatians 6:7 (KJV), Be not deceived God is not mocked: for whatsoever a man soweth, that shall he also reap.*

Luke 6:38 (KJV), Give, and it shall be given unto you; good measure, pressed down, and shaken together, and running over, shall men give into your bosom. For with the same measure that ye mete withal it shall be measured to you again.

Wealth is based on covenant relationship. Anything in the life of a believer procured outside of the direction of the Holy Spirit is selfish gain.

Power Key: *Increase Without Agreement Is Selfish Gain.*

I John 5:4, For whatever is born of God is victorious over the world: and this is the victory that conquers

188 ~ Thomas Michael

the world, even our faith. I am convinced that either you agree with what God wants you to have or you produce what you want of the flesh. I have determined not to make any purchases without the consent and blessing of the Lord. Make a decision, within yourself, not to make another purchase without consulting the Holy Spirit. God cannot entrust His people with His Wealth until they have shown themselves to be faithful stewards. Stewardship is more than just understanding the principles of tithing and managing your personal finances.

Everything! Everything! Everything your heart desires, God is willing to give you. It is His nature and His character. It thrills God to bless you. Remember, God loves a cheerful giver. A cheerful giver is one whom God has blessed. It is one whose joy comes from giving, because of their abundance. *Acts 20:35b (KJV), ...and to remember the words of the Lord Jesus, how He said, "it is more blessed to give than to receive."* Giving is a form of your worship to the Lord. The more you give the more of His presence you unlock.

Power Key: ***The Product Of True Worship Is The Fulfillment Of Desire.***

Psalm 37:4, Delight yourself in the Lord, and He will give you the desires and secret petitions of your heart.

Worship is delighting in the Lord. When you delight yourself in the Lord, you automatically, due to the intimacy of worship, reveal the secrets of your heart. There is nothing hidden. God is Omniscient, all knowing, there is nothing we can hide from Him. He knows the intent of our hearts and its desires as well. *Proverbs 22:4, The reward of humility and the reverent and worshipful fear of the Lord is riches and honor and life.*

Power Key: ***In The Intimacy Of Worship, The Secrets Of The Heart Are Revealed.***

Humility is an inward characteristic and is the catalyst for true worship. Worship positions your heart in righteousness making you a candidate for the Wealth of God. Wealth can only be transferred and entrusted to people with right motives of the heart. God will not give you something that could become an obstacle. A heart that is free from offense and flowing in agreement is the first prerequisite for a Wealth transfer. *II Chronicles 1:11,12, God replied to Solomon, because this was in your heart and you have not asked for riches, possessions, honor and glory, or the life of your foes, or even for long life, but have asked wisdom and knowledge for yourself, that you may rule and judge My people over whom I have made you king, wisdom and knowledge are granted you. And I will give you riches, possessions, honor, and glory, such as none of the kings had before you, and none after you shall have their equal.*

Solomon's reward for not asking the Lord to bless him with riches was Wealth beyond his imagination.

You are probably thinking to yourself that this applies to men of God or people in the Bible only. God has a plan for placing His Wealth in the hands of trustworthy believers. *Ecclesiastes 5:19, Every man also to*

*whom God hath given riches and wealth, and hath given him power to eat thereof, and to take his portion, and to rejoice in his labor; **this is the gift of God**.* Wealth is a gift from God. It is apparent in the verbiage used in this passage, "…and to rejoice in his labor," pleasure in your labor is automatic when you become so abundantly blessed.

There is a Wealth transfer taking place in the Spirit. Are you ready? Ask God to forgive you of any offenses, any bitterness in your heart. Choose to walk in agreement and find the agreeable factor in every situation.

Prayer of Agreement:

Heavenly Father, God of Covenant Agreement, I come before You today. I ask You to forgive me of my offenses. Take away the bitterness and heal me of the rejection. I want Your Wealth. I will be a good steward. I pray in complete agreement with Your Spirit. In the Name of the Father, the Son, Jesus, and the Holy Spirit.

Amen

Power Keys:

~The Power Of Wealth Is The Means Of Influence To The World.
~Agreement Is The Most Powerful Force In The Universe By Its Very Nature.
~Wealth Is God's Reward For Agreement.
~The Essence Of Wisdom Is Unlocked Through The

Humility Of Worshipful Fear.
~Worship Unlocks The Wealth Of God.
~Desire Is Clothed In The Vesture Of Worship.
~Worship Incites God's Desire Toward Us.
~The Anointing Of Agreement Breaks The Yoke Of Bondage Of Anything Agreed Upon.
~Where There Is Agreement There Is Abundance.
~Increase Without Agreement Is Selfish Gain.
~The Product Of True Worship Is The Fulfillment Of Desire.
~In The Intimacy Of Worship The Secrets Of The Heart Are Revealed.

~13~

WRONG PEOPLE

Power Key: *Agreement With Right People Produces Success; Agreement With Wrong People Produces Failure.*

braham was called the friend of God and was known for his righteous ways. Still, he allowed his nephew to follow him into a right season of his life and it cost him. The Bible states, in the Book of I Corinthians, *not to be deceived and misled! Evil companionships and associations corrupt and deprave good manners, morals and character.* Although Lot was not a bad person in Abraham's life; he was a carrier of rebellion, contention, and strife. The very meaning of Lot's name reveals the disease he carried. Lot means *"veil, disobedience, inattentive, mishear, neglectful to hear."*

Deceptive and inattentive as Lot was, Abraham still allowed him to accompany him, because he was family.

Are you harboring a fugitive? Have you carried an infectious, diseased individual into the next season of your life, because you felt sorry for him? You must sever that relationship immediately. If you do not separate yourself from the "Lots" in your life, they will cost you greatly.

Every person, in your life, will either draw you close to God's presence and His blessings, or will be a carrier of the infectious disease called "rebellion." No believer is strong enough to override a rebellious attitude; the rebellious will eventually affect the obedient.

Power Key: *Sin Is Contagious; Holiness Is Not!*

Rebellion is a spirit; rooted, entangled and birthed out of pride. Lucifer created rebellion. It was an invention of his jealousy, envy and pride. It existed before our world was ever created. *Rebellion is a stronghold; it was birthed from the bowels of polluted worship and is a mockery of worship itself.*

Rebellion is an inward trait; it is not always evident on the countenance. Lucifer was offering up polluted worship to God; he was saying with his lips, "Yes, God, I will worship You and You alone." Moreover, on the inside he was saying, "I will make myself like You, the Most High." How many times have you said to your superior, "Yes, I will…" with your lips, but on the inside you were saying, "I will do it this time, but I'll make you pay." *Matthew 15:8 (KJV), This people draweth nigh*

unto me with their mouth, and honoreth me with their lips; but their heart is far from me. But in vain they do worship me, teaching for doctrines the commandments of men.

You may be able to quote Scripture and have a good confession. You may have received a word or vision from God. However, unless you are connected to right people, God's plan cannot be carried out in your life. There are divine connections in your life you may be overlooking, perhaps, because of their appearance. Do not be dismayed; God will open your eyes and enable you to recognize who they are. More importantly, you must be sharper in discerning who is ***not*** a divine connection.

You will always gravitate to the wrong connection quicker than you will to the right connection. Your physical discerners, called "eyes," will automatically see things that can link you to Wrong People. Your eyes cannot be the source for discovering God's assigned people for your life.

I purposely chose to write the chapter about Wrong People first, before I wrote the chapter about right people. I am keenly aware of the pull of the flesh that will quickly persuade you to connect with Wrong People. Abraham looked to the obvious to discover who would go with him into the next level where God would take him.

Power Key: *Is It A Good Thing Or A God Thing?*

I mentioned earlier, Lot was not a bad "thing" in Abraham's life, but was he a "God" thing? There will be many times when, within your own intellect, you will conceive "good" ideas. Consequently, these ideas are not always "God" ideas. Find out what God's mind and thoughts are in every situation. That is the premise for this entire book; find the agreeable factor in every situation. The agreeable factor must be what God's Spirit desires. Dr. Murdock writes in his masterpiece of a book, The Law of Recognition, *"When you tolerate the presence of those who are rebellious against God, you will taste the same results and consequences."*

Abraham had to experience the sting of Lot's rebellion and deception. It was then, that he recognized his problems were linked to a wrong person in his life. How difficult it must have been for Abraham to decide that the removal of his own family member would be the difference between success and failure. There is nothing you agree to walk away from that God will not bring back to you on His terms.

Perhaps, you can think of a wrong connection in your life; maybe, a relative, a friend, or a co-worker. You must decide to disconnect from people who are not content to do the will of God.

Power Key: *Disconnect From The Discontented.*

God will never place you in a position that compromises His assignment for your life. This is the obvious work of a more cunning entity, and I am not talking about the devil.

Jesus said, "Behold, I give you power over all the power of the devil." The devil is no longer a threat.

There is a cunningness that works as much against you operating in agreement as God's desire for you to live victoriously. Much of the opposition we face in life is straightforwardly related to our choices. You must choose who to agree with and who not to; and choose which voice you listen to.

Power Key: *Life Is A Sequence Of Choices; The Quality Of That Life Is Contingent Upon The Consistency Of Right Choices.*

Somewhere along the way, the Holy Spirit spoke His direction to you, but you did not hear Him. The Holy Spirit is continually consulting with every believer on every decision.

Genesis 13:13 (KJV), But the men of Sodom were wicked and sinners before the Lord exceedingly sinful. This Scripture reveals the nature of Lot. He made a choice based on his sinful intrigue. It is evident that Lot's choice was fraught with failure when the destiny of Sodom and Gomorrah was finally played out. While Lot was not a participant of the evil debauchery that was so prevalent in Sodom and Gomorrah, he remained long enough for his own children to become entangled. Lot's children were eventually infected with the sinful ways of Sodom and Gomorrah and ended up committing incest with Lot. As I am writing this chapter, I have just realized the topic of wrong connections has fallen aptly on Chapter 13. The passage found in Genesis 13:13 is as much a confirmation of the destructive results of a wrong connection. According to the book by Kevin J. Conner,

Interpreting The Symbols and Types, the number 13 means apostasy, backsliding and rebellion. (I am not a big numerology fan; this is strictly coincidental.)

How do you know if you are connecting with Wrong People? The fruit of every relationship will eventually yield the sweetness of ripened fruit or the stench of rotten, unidentifiable fruit. Do not waste your time on an Ishmael; guard your time for the season when your Isaac appears.

Power Key: *We Must Lower Our Expectations Of People And Raise Our Expectations Of God.*

If you are anything like me, you have probably had relationships you were convinced were divine connections, only to be shocked beyond your wildest imagination when they made their surprise exit. It will not be too long, after you have sifted through a couple of sour relationships that your discernment will become much keener.

God has divine connections for your life. You must decide to become a divine connection for others as well.

God places people on the same path in life to help one another and, yet, so many abort the plan and "divorce" their divine connections. I am truly convinced God has put people together whose lives depend on the right connection. At some point, these individuals will need one who can help them; however, since they have cut out the person who could deliver them, their lives could be cut short. Nothing is by chance; it is by choice. God gave us the power to choose. Nothing is by accident; it is a result of decisions and choices.

The Church, somewhere along the way, allowed offense to strip it of its very strength, *covenant agreement.* Without the power to heal and strengthen relationships, what difference does the Church celebrate from the world? The world is plagued by divorce, separation, and mistrust; who, but the Church can heal it?

Agreement eliminates the shiftiness of relationships which is a reflection of the world's standard of conduct. Do not become desensitized by the customs of this world, thus diluting the potency of relationships within God's kingdom. The world functions completely on the premise of wrong connections, because they are not covenant people. When everyone is wrong, every connection is wrong. Only people of covenant may have divine connections. *Titus 1:15 (KJV), Unto the pure all things are pure: but unto them that are defiled and unbelieving is nothing pure; but even their mind and conscience are defiled.*

You must use the standard of God's Word as your guide for right relationships. Agreement then becomes the glue that binds two people together for life, regardless of the hardships and moments of mistrust.

Power Key: *Agreement Looks Beyond What Is And Sees What Will Be.*

There are numerous examples of men and women, in the Scripture, who came into agreement with the Wrong People.

Samson's demise was not based on his inability to

keep a promise with God. His purpose was to destroy the Philistines; in the very end, he does just that. In the meantime, he connects with Wrong People. Samson had a most unprofitable handicap when it came to choosing relationships. He had three different lovers and they were all traders or harlots. You only need one Delilah to destroy your destiny. *Judges 14:3, But his father and mother said to him, is there not a woman among the daughters of your kinsmen or among all our people, that you must go to take a wife from the uncircumcised Philistines? And Samson said to his father, get her for me, for she is alright in my eyes.* Despite his parent's plea to choose a wife from among their own people, Samson makes his decision based on what he sees. I mentioned earlier, your first inclination before choosing a divine connection is usually based on looks. Incidentally, your destiny is connected to divine connections and the absence of wrong relationships. You may have a wonderful relationship with your pastor, and he may counsel you to disconnect from a potentially dangerous relationship. If you do not obey his instruction, it will negate your relationship with him.

II King 5:15b,16,20,25-27 (KJV), ...So now accept a gift from your servant. Elisha said, as the Lord lives, before Whom I stand, I will accept none. He urged him to take it, but Elisha refused. But Gehazi, the servant of Elisha the man of God, said, Behold, my master spared this Naaman the Syrian, in not receiving from his hands what he brought. But as the Lord lives, I will run after him and get something from him. He went in and stood before his master. Elisha said, where have you been

Gehazi? He said, your servant went nowhere. Elisha said to him, did not my spirit go with you when the man turned from his chariot to meet you? Was it a time to accept money, garments, olive orchards, vineyards, sheep, oxen, menservants, and maidservants? Therefore the leprosy of Naaman shall cleave to you and to your off-spring forever. And Gehazi went from his presence a leper as white as snow. Elisha ministered healing to Naaman, but knew not to have any association with him, regardless of his stature and wealth.

Power Key: ***The Bitter Root Of Offense Is A Matter Of Life And Death.***

Naaman had come to Israel, clad with great wealth, prepared to pay a physician for treatment. Elisha would not come close to Naaman per God's instruction. The Syrian commander, Naaman, was puffed up and haughty and easily insulted. He was quickly offended when the man of God did not come to where he was, wave his "anointed" hand, and banish the leprosy. When Elisha sent instruction for Naaman's healing, he directed him to the muddy banks of the Jordan River. Naaman was too proud to dip in the Jordan and suggested two other more suitable rivers. He stormed off in a rage, but his armor-bearers calmed him down and he received his healing nonetheless.

Naaman went back to the prophet's house, no doubt, humbled. He wanted to reward Elisha and confess his conversion. Elisha refused his gifts, blessed him and sent him on his way. He was definitely a Wrong Person to connect with regardless of his generosity because of his enemy status against Israel. A relationship with an enemy of God's people is a violation of the covenant agreement. *Exodus 23:22 (KJV), But if thou shalt indeed obey His voice, and do all that I speak; then I will be an enemy unto thine enemies, and adversary unto thine adversaries.* If God keeps no alliance with our enemies, neither should we keep company with the enemies of our covenant brothers.

Elisha's armor-bearer, Gehazi, followed after the commander's chariot. He got too close to the enemy of God, and the glimmer and shine of Naaman's wealth seduced him. He approached the commander and made a deceptive request on behalf of Elisha. He asked for $1920.00 and two Giorgio Armani suits supposedly for the sons of some prophets that were coming to town. When Gehazi stood before Elisha, the Prophet asked him, "Where have you been?" Gehazi replies, "I have gone no where." Elisha rebukes him saying, "Was not my spirit with you when you went after the commander?" Elisha speaks a curse upon Gehazi, pronouncing him a leper for life and his descendants as well. Gehazi's agreement with Naaman cost him greatly.

Power Key: *Violation Of Agreement With A Man Of God Sets In Motion The Process Of Death.*

It is imperative for you to understand the damaging effects of one wrong person in your life. You may think I am being a bit overdramatic. A particular incident comes to mind of a man I knew quite well. His destiny was very promising, both financially and in ministry. I remember giving him a directive from the Lord to stay away from an untrustworthy individual, but he refused it. He now lives in misery, incarcerated by his own choices.

Pray over your relationships and test them against what the Spirit wants for your life.

Ask yourself:

- Does this person permit me to hold on to fleshly things?
- Does this person increase or decrease my life?
- Is this person a part of my assignment?
- Do I look to this person as my source? (Financially, emotionally, spiritually)

Prayer of Agreement:

Holy Spirit, More than any other person in my life, I need You. Please help me to make right choices, and choose only those people You have assigned in my life. Give me wisdom and courage to remove myself from Wrong People. In the Name of Jesus I pray,

Amen.

Power Keys:

~Agreement With Right People Produces Success; Agreement With Wrong People Produces Failure.
~Sin Is Contagious Holiness Is Not.
~Is It A Good Thing Or God Thing?
~Disconnect From The Discontented.
~Life Is A Sequence Of Choices; The Quality Of That

Life Is Contingent Upon The Consistency Of Right Choices.

~We Must Lower Our Expectations Of People And Raise Our Expectations Of God.

~Agreement Looks Beyond What Is And Sees What Will Be.

~The Bitter Root Of Offense Is A Matter Of Life And Death.

~Violation Of Agreement With A Man Of God Sets In Motion The Process Of Death.

~14~

Right People

Power Key: *Agreement With Right People Creates A Clearer Picture Of The Future.*

 hat is the difference between a right and wrong relationship? To begin with, a right connection is only right if agreement is at its root. Agreement is not the shrinkage of life, rather, the expansion of life. There is not a relationship on this earth that ever was or ever will be, that can exist or survive outside of agreement. There can be no lasting relationship outside of agreement. Remember, it was agreement before it was love.

A prerequisite for coming into agreement with Right People is to eliminate wrong people. *Proverbs 13:20, He who walks [as a companion] with wise men is*

wise, but he who associates with [self confident] fools is [a fool himself and] shall smart for it. Right People help you get to where you are going. Wrong people eventually prove to be a hindrance. The divinely connected help complete a puzzle that reveals a picture of your future, thus making the journey much more enjoyable. Agreement with Right People is the only way to travel on the cruise liner of life. You may be able to get on the boat, but you do not enjoy the trip if you are in the wrong room with the wrong person. It would be like taking your life's journey on a Greyhound bus, instead of charting through the waters of life on the Princess Cruise Liner. The romance of life requires the support of only those called to strengthen and carry the lover's burdens.

Power Key: ***The Mastery Of Agreement Is Found In Your Decision To Become A Willing Participant.***

How does one master the art of agreement? It is as simple as being a willing participant. You cannot expect Right People to come into your life if you are not striving to be a right person yourself. If every believer would endeavor to be a person of excellence and a right person, there would be no trouble connecting with Right People!

Power Key: ***Your Response To People Around You Is A Reflection Of How You See Yourself.***

Eliminate the wrong people to focus on the right. Someone out there needs you; their success is dependent upon you. God will allow your paths to cross. Will you be able to recognize that individual? Remember, it is not based on what you see; it is based on your willingness to help others carry out their dream. Do not worry thinking all your time will only be used to help someone else fulfill their dream. *Luke 6:38 (KJV), Give, and it shall be given unto you; good measure, pressed down, and shaken together, and running over, shall men give into your bosom. For with the same measure that ye mete withal it shall be measured to you again.* You can never out-give what God gives to you. Agreement finds its existence in the covenant blessings of God. It is about "making a deal" that causes good things to happen for you when you make them happen for others. Agreement is assurance of victory!

Matthew 26:25, Peter said to Him, even if I must die with You, I will not deny or disown You! And all the disciples said the same thing. You must be willing to die to hold on to a divine connection. Jesus did not have time to waste on people who could not help him carry out His life's assignment. Can you imagine Jesus standing before the Father, attempting to make excuses for the deferment of His assignment to Calvary because of whiny individuals? Agreement with Right People will put you at the right place, right on schedule. Although, the disciples could not see exactly where Jesus was going, He had each one of their moves calculated down to the wire. *Luke 22:10-13, He said to them, behold, when you have gone into the city, a man carrying an earthen jug or pitcher of water will meet you: follow him into the house which he enters, and say to the master of the house, the*

teacher asks you, where is the guest room, where I may eat the Passover [meal] with my disciples? And he will show you a large room upstairs, furnished [with carpets and with couches properly spread]; There make[your] preparations. And they went and found it [just] as He had said to them; and they made ready the Passover [supper].

The care to detail, in this incident, is quite astounding. In those days, only women carried water pitchers and men carried wineskins. *God will make it obvious with whom you are to agree, even if He has to put a pitcher of water on his head.*

Notwithstanding, there will be people in your life whose assignment will be for a brief season. The disciples' connection with the servant carrying the pitcher of water was only for a moment. Yet, he was instrumental in the process of this historical moment when Jesus and His disciples partook of the Last Supper. Without this seemingly, insignificant individual, God's master plan would not have unfolded.

What if the servant carrying the water decided he should be the only star in his life's drama? What if he had not yielded to God's master plan? Perchance, he could have copped an attitude about walking downtown in public view with a pitcher of water in his hands. Right People cannot always be number one, even when performing on their own stage. John the Baptist could never have been number one, because he was called to prepare the way for the Messiah, Jesus Christ. My executive assistant, Melanie, has purposed in her heart to be the number "1" number "2" person; and that she is. That is the nature of agreement.

Matthew 26:26-28, Now as they were eating, Jesus took bread and, praising God, gave thanks and asked Him to bless it to their use, and when He had broken it, He gave it to the disciples and said, take, eat; this is My Body. And He took a cup, and when He had given thanks, He gave it to them, saying, Drink of it, all of you; for this is My blood of the new covenant, which [ratifies the agreement and] is being poured out for many for the forgiveness of sins. Jesus was calling His disciples to renew their agreement with Him by sharing the Passover Supper together. He was making a salute to agreement. He raised a glass of wine, in commemoration of the occasion, and made the act of agreement visible through the Last Supper. All of this transpired on the eve of the Passover. Jesus wanted to know who would stay in the agreement with him through the thick of the battle. He wanted to know who the Right People in His life were. Communion is a renewal of the covenant agreement with Christ as our Passover Lamb.

How can you know who is a right person in your life? By their willingness to remain in agreement when you walk through the storms of your life.

RIGHT PEOPLE WILL...
~Defend you in your absence.
~Make your enemies their enemies.
~Adjust their plans to conform to your needs.
~Use discretion.
~Embrace your dreams.
~Rejoice when you are rewarded.
~Cover your weaknesses.

~*The Proof Of Love Is Loyalty*~

The importance, relevance and desperation for agreement is summed up in the passage, "This do in remembrance of me…" In other words, Jesus was saying, "Remain loyal to my teaching and thus, prove your love for me." Agreement is not an option for the believer. It is the way of the righteous. God told Abraham to walk before Him blameless. He was saying, ***"Abraham, stay in the agreement."***

The disciples were divinely connected to Christ in many ways. They were committed to His teaching and His call. *Matthew 16:24 (KJV), If any man will come after Me, let him deny himself, and take up his cross and follow Me...* These words are the epitome of agreement. Where is the confusion in this verbiage? If any man will deny himself… This is the act of agreement: laying down your dreams and embracing the dreams of another. Jesus was asking His followers to take up His cross, His dreams, His mission. How can believers, in supposedly good membership-status, deny their pastor's vision and push their own ideas? This violates the law of agreement and only yields disaster.

A godly individual is one who can walk away from his/her dreams and embrace the dreams of another. Are you a divine connection for someone?

Although, I have already written about the astonishing rapport between Ruth and Naomi, I would be remiss in not expounding a little more while writing the chapter of agreement with Right People.

If there were ever two "un-right" people for each other, it would have to be a daughter-in-law and a mother-in-law. How often do you see mother-in-laws embracing their son's wife and agreeing to let her move in; especially after the son is already dead? It is truly a rarity.

The famous monologue of agreement, found in the Book of Ruth, is more than a nice little quote to be used at weddings and such. It is the cornerstone for every right relationship. *Ruth 1:16-17, And Ruth said, urge me not to leave you or to turn back from following you: for where you go I will go, and where you lodge I will lodge, your people shall be my people and your God my God. Where you die I will die, and there will I be buried. The Lord do so to me and more also, if anything but death parts me from you.*

It is clear from the outcome of this agreement that Ruth ended up with a husband with whom she would have to make a similar agreement. So, what happened to her agreement with Naomi? It lived on, because Ruth's husband Boaz embraced Naomi and provided for her as well.

Naomi had two daughter's-in-law; yet, only one receives the honor of a book in the Bible with her name-sake. The other daughter-in-law, Orpah, was given the same opportunity to follow Naomi. Instead, taking her destiny into her own hands, she returned to the people of her gods.

Most people would have agreed with Orpah on her decision not to link up with a cantankerous old woman. The obvious would have been to separate from an unforgiving, offended person, who even asked to change her name from Naomi to *Mara*, which means bitterness. In the light of such self-pity and self-deprecation, Ruth still clings to Naomi, cursing herself if she miscarries the agreement with Naomi.

It was the anointing of agreement flowing through Ruth which provides the much needed healing and deliverance for Naomi. Your agreeable spirit will produce an anointing which can free people from offense. The Bible says, we are called to be repairers of the breach.

Power Key: *Agreement Is The Binding Force To Any Successful Relationship.*

Ask yourself the following questions:

- Do I need this person to help fulfill my dreams?
- Does this person need me to fulfill their dreams?
- Is this person moving me towards God's presence or away?
- Is this person willing to embrace the dreams of the one in authority over me?
- Is this person a part of my solution?
- Do they create distractions or focus in my life?

PRAYER OF AGREEMENT:

Dear Lord Jesus, I ask You to take away the wrong people in my life and show me the right ones. Please give me an obvious sign and show me who they are. I know that my connection with Right People will result in my success. In the Name of the Father, the Son, and the Holy Ghost.

Amen

POWER KEYS:

~Agreement With Right People Creates A Clearer Picture Of The Future.
~The Mastery Of Agreement Is Found In Your Decision To Become A Willing Participant.
~Your ResponseTo People Around You Is A Reflection Of How You See Yourself.
~The Proof Of Love Is Loyalty.
~Agreement Is The Binding Force To Any Successful Relationship.

~15~

ONE TO AGREE WITH

Power Key: *The Power For Winning Is Connected To The People God Assigns To You.*

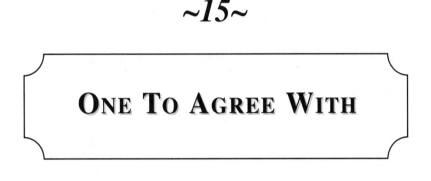very man of God has been given the privilege of mentoring others while increasing his own chances of winning in life. The more right people in one's life, the higher the stakes for winning. *Matthew 16:24, Then Jesus said to His disciples, If anyone desires to be My disciple, let him deny himself [disregard, lose sight of, and forget himself and his own interest] and take up his cross and follow Me [cleave steadfastly to Me, conform wholly to My example in living and, if need be, in dying also].*

A man of God with a right Armor-bearer has the confidence of knowing he has *one to agree with at all*

times. An Armor-bearer is available at any time to agree with the man of God, even when those closest to him have difficulty agreeing. *I Samuel 14:7, And his armor-bearer said to him, do all that is in your mind: I am with you in whatever you think [best].* The Armor-bearer stands with his man of God regardless! He is one who carries, stirs up, completes, finishes, protects, brings to pass, bears up, respects and yields to his man of God.

An Armor-bearer is much like a golfer's caddie. Tiger Woods, the great, young, black, pro-golfer, has a caddie who must know as much about the game as Tiger does. The caddie has the same knowledge as the pro-golfer, even though he does not possess the same abilities. He is able to discern what wood or what iron the golfer should use to execute an intended shot.

The Armor-bearer has the same virtue; he is one who completes or overlaps where the man of God is not able. He is not your typical sheep in the fold; he is more like a German shepherd. He is the watchdog for the man and woman of God. The old adage, "A dog is a man's best friend" rings true for the Armor-bearer. He protects and scares away unwanted visitors. He loves unconditionally and above all, is always trainable.

Power Key: *Training Is The Enforcement Of Doing What You Already Know.*

There is a big difference between teaching and training. In most churches there is no shortage on teaching, however, many have little or no training for people with an Armor-bearer calling.

Basic training for the Armor-bearer must begin before he ever approaches the man of God. The first lesson being servanthood. It is never the responsibility of the man of God to train an Armor-bearer; it is the job of another Armor-bearer. An archer can only instruct another archer.

An Armor-bearer must be mature enough to handle the instructions he receives from the man of God. Contrarily, he may become too familiar and grow to resent the leader. Herein lies the biggest problem I have encountered in my relationships with Armor-bearers; I have tried to train in an area that I am not called nor well versed in.

If you are called to be an Armor-bearer, you must learn how to serve a man or woman of God in a way that helps them maximize their talents, anointings, and ministries. You must always comply with the posture of agreement which is humility.

Power Key: *If You Walk In Humility, You Will Never Be Humiliated.*

The Armor-bearer who clothes himself with the vesture of servanthood will always find himself in a subordinate position with the man of God. The moment he feels he is his equal, he has breached the agreement between master and servant, between scholar and student.

~The Difference Between An Armor-bearer And A Protégé~

There is a unique difference between an Armor bearer and a Protégé. The Armor-bearer has no promise of becoming his mentor's successor. This is where many Armor-bearers miss the call. They look to their mentors with admiration, yet confused, they desire the position of the leader because of its glamour and glory. A true Armor-bearer does not desire the position of his pastor or mentor; he is satisfied and content to serve, knowing that his reward comes from a source other than the man of God. The only exception is the time when David was Saul's Armor-bearer, in which case, God intervened and anointed David to be king.

An Armor-bearer's calling is equally as important as a Protégé's. Some have interpreted the position of a protégé as higher than that of an Armor-bearer who is looked upon as a mere servant. The position of a Protégé is simply that of a glorified Armor-bearer, except that the requirements are greater. *God picks a Protégé from among the ripened fruit of the tree of servanthood.*

The Protégé must serve the man of God with a greater level of humility, knowing that one day he could succeed him. An Armor-bearer has no hope or aspiration for his mentor's position.

A Protégé must always remain in absolute agreement with his mentor. There are always plenty of others who disagree with the man of God. He is so close to his leader that when God speaks, God's voice sounds like his mentor. *I Samuel 3:4-9, When the Lord called, Samuel!*

And he answered, here I am. He ran to Eli and said, Here I am, for you called me. Eli said, I did not call you; lie down again. So he went and lay down. And the Lord called again, Samuel! And Samuel arose and went to Eli and said, Here am I; you did call me. Eli answered, I did not call, my son; lie down again. Now Samuel did not yet know the Lord, and the word of the Lord was not yet revealed to him. And the Lord called Samuel the third time. And he went to Eli and said, Here I am, for you did call me. Then Eli perceived that the Lord was calling the boy. So Eli said to Samuel, go, lie down. And if He calls you, you shall say, speak, Lord, for Your servant is listening. So Samuel went and lay down in his place.

Samuel was Eli's Protégé and was in such unity and agreement with him that God's voice sounded just like his master's.

A man encounters difficulty in becoming an Armor-bearer or a Protégé if he has not first served his own father. This has become the nemesis for most men who desire to be mentored by a man of God. They have not yet, learned to submit to their earthly fathers; therefore, it becomes virtually impossible for them to submit to a spiritual father. While different situations prevent some men from having a successful father-son relationship, the criteria to be met are not found in the success of the relationship, rather, in the ability to serve "a man." It matters not whether he is an alcoholic father, an uncle, an older brother, or a coach.

My father was an alcoholic; yet, everything I am I owe to him. He gave me my ingenuity for business, taught me about hard work, taught me to be a man of my word, and demanded the highest respect. The "absent father" in the homes of America is costing our country far more than we realize. Now, we as the Church, are called to fill the vacancy of fatherhood by providing mentorship programs and ministries.

The anointing of an Armor-bearer is significantly different from a Protégé's. God anoints and calls an Armor-bearer; a man of God places his anointing upon the Protégé. *Numbers 11:17, And I will come down and talk with you there: and I will take of the spirit which is upon you and will put it upon them: and they shall bear the burden of the people with you, so that you may not have to bear it yourself alone.*

My assistant pastor and I were talking the other day. We spoke of the attacks of Satan on people's lives that have a great impact on society. We both agreed, since Satan is not omnipresent nor omniscient, he cannot be at all places at the same time. Therefore, most Christians have probably not had an encounter with Satan himself. He said, "I don't think I've had to encounter Satan." I shared with him, how persuaded I was, that he would never have to meet the devil. I have fought and sustained many attacks from Satan in my lifetime. Since I have defeated the devil, he only has to remain in agreement with me, until such a time, when I lay my hands upon him and transfer my anointing. He then becomes eligible to become my successor. God comes down by His Spirit and places the same spirit of the man of God upon the Armor-bearer.

~The Humility Of An Armor-bearer~

David, Saul, Jonathan, and Abimelech all had Armor-bearers; yet, none of these Armor-bearers were listed by name in the Scriptures. This implies there was a deep trait of humility among the Armor-bearers of that day. How much more shall humility be evident in the servants of today with the enrichment of the fruit of the Holy Spirit?

~The Calling Of A Protégé~

Most people have interpreted Elijah and Elisha's relationship as one of an Armor-bearer and man of God; on the contrary, Elisha was Elijah's Protégé.

The Protégé has the benefit of becoming his mentor's successor, provided he remains in the agreement until the delegation of office takes place. He is one who is called to support the man of God, enabling him to have a further reach by becoming an extension of the pastor. Wherever the man of God is, the Protégé should be present. *II Kings 2:2, And Elijah said to Elisha, tarry here, I pray you, for the Lord has sent me to Bethel. But Elisha replied, as the Lord lives and as your soul lives, I will not leave you. So they went down to Bethel.* Three times in the following verses Elijah bids Elisha to stay put, but Elisha refuses to be separated from his master. Elijah was testing his servant to see if he would remain in the agreement.

A Protégé learns by watching his mentor, not only through instruction, but by example.

Power Key: *The Anointing Of A Mentor And A Protégé Is The Same Because It Flows From The Head Down.*

Deuteronomy 34:9, And Joshua son of Nun was full of the spirit of wisdom, for Moses had laid his hands upon him: so the Israelites listened to him and did as the Lord commanded Moses. While Joshua was speaking to the children of Israel, they were still carrying out Moses' instruction. That is right order!

Power Key: *The Peace Of Immediate Obedience Is Always Greater Than The Comfort Of Deferred Obedience.*

When a Protégé's focus is on his own agenda and his message does not coincide with the man of God, he violates protocol, thus creating disorder among the subordinates. The Protégé then ties his own hands, making his efforts and labor ineffective.

A man of God's productivity is easily stifled and hindered when a Protégé and/or an Armor-bearer questions the policies of procedure for ministry. Their actions imply the one in charge is incompetent. Their comments can turn manipulative and create broken focus.

When the prophet Samuel anointed David to be king, he did not run out and begin his worldwide ministry. Instead, he returned in submission to his father and remained in his original agreement to tend the smelly sheep. David did not move out until it was time.

Power Key: *When Authority Yields To Servanthood, It Is Called Witchcraft.*

The whole gambit becomes entrenched in witch-craft when a Protégé or an Armor-bearer thinks he can excel above the mentor. By witchcraft, I mean anything that flows from the bottom up is cloaked in rebellion and will result in manipulation and struggle for control.

I have submitted myself to a physical trainer who is qualified to train. Whatever Guy says, in the realm of health and nutrition, is what goes. I am very submitted to his training in the field of fitness, because it is his expert-ise. Recently, God called me to a 96-hour worship marathon and I was out of the gym for an entire week. My trainer stayed out of the gym in respect for my posi-tion as his pastor. His honor for me would not allow him to advance without me. That is right order!

Perhaps, you feel a call to be an Armor-bearer. The qualifications for becoming an Armor-bearer are simply having a readiness to humbly serve the man of God and remaining in agreement by embodying the char-acteristics of Christ. Terry Nance says, "The spirit of an armor-bearer is the spirit of Christ." What kind of spirit did Jesus exude when He walked on this earth? He was a meek, humble, agreeable man. He carried the weight of the world on His shoulders and was the epitome of an Armor-bearer.

PRAYER OF AGREEMENT:

Dear Lord Jesus, I aspire to be like You. Give me

the strength to carry the burden of the things in my family's life and in my church that You would have me carry. Place within me a spirit of humility and willingness to be an Armor-bearer to others in agreement. In the Name of the Father, the Son, Jesus, and the Holy Spirit.

Amen

POWER KEYS:

~The Power For Winning Is Connected To The People God Assigns To You.

~Training Is The Enforcement Of Doing What You Already Know.

~If You Walk In Humility, You Will Never Be Humiliated.

~The Anointing Of A Mentor And A Protégé Is The Same Because It Flows From The Head Down.

~The Peace Of Immediate Obedience Is Always Greater Than The Comfort Of Deferred Obedience.

~When Authority Yields To Servanthood, It Is Called Witchcraft.

~16~

THE BLOOD COVENANT

Power Key: *Relationships Were Made For Agreement.*

elationships are equipped with an automatic support system. When you fall, there is always someone to pick you up. When you are cold, someone is there to warm you. In the heat of battle, someone is there to fight along side you. *Ecclesiastes 4:9-12, [Two are better than one, because they have a good] more satisfying reward for their labor; for if they fall, the one will lift up his fellow. But woe to him who is alone when he falls and has not another to lift him up! Again, if two lie down together, then they have warmth; but how can one be warm alone? And though a man might prevail against him who is alone, two will withstand him. A threefold*

cord is not quickly broken.

"Where do I begin to tell the story of how great a love can be?" so goes the theme song from the movie, Love Story. It is the scene for the "perfect love" between a man and a woman. One of the legendary lines from the movie is, "Love is never having to say you're sorry." That sounds more like a line from the manual on Agreement (if there was one.) The characters in this love story receive their strength during the course of the woman's bout with cancer, which eventually takes her life. Every relationship that moves beyond the obvious attractions of the exterior person will eventually undergo a transformation resulting in a supernatural strengthening.

Power Key: ***Agreement Looks Beyond What Is And Sees What Will Be.***

A relationship founded on the Gibraltar of Agreement goes beyond the feelings and hardships of reciprocal relationship and ultimately beyond this age. Agreement is the Church's grooming for eternity. The agreement of earthly relationships is the preparation for walking in agreement with the divinity of the Godhead.

Power Key: ***Agreement Is The Binding Force To Any Successful Relationship.***

God designed every relationship you encounter for agreement: the good, the bad, and the ugly. I want to focus mainly on the positive relationships in your life. Nevertheless, agreement with your enemy is making concession for God to give you victory. There can be no victory without a battle. God uses the repugnant, bitter taste of your enemies to give you a comparison of the blessing of His sovereign relationships for your life.

Matthew 5:25 (KJV), Agree with thine adversary quickly, whiles thou art in the way with him; lest at any time the adversary deliver thee to the judge, and the judge deliver thee to the officer, and thou be cast into prison. Agreement with an enemy can mean the difference between a lawsuit and just walking away from an idiot. Never fight a battle without the benefit of reward. What good is fighting if it is not for increase and for a positive outcome?

Psalm 133:1-3, Behold, how good and how pleasant it is for brethren to dwell together in unity! It is like the precious ointment poured on the head, that ran down the beard, even the beard of Aaron [the first high priest], that came down upon the collar and skirts of his garments [consecrating the whole body], it is like the dew of [lofty] Mount Hermon and the dew that comes on the hills of Zion; for there the Lord has commanded the blessing, even life forevermore [upon the high and the lowly].

Relationships were made for agreement! It is one of the pleasantries of unity. When people walk together in agreement, the visual picture the Psalmist received was of the lofty, strong Mount Hermon covered with dew. Can you picture a mountain glistening with the sun's rays as every petal on every flower shimmers with the morning dew? Agreement is beautiful! The Scripture says, "...for *there* the Lord commanded the blessing." *"There"* meaning in agreement. Allow me to paraphrase Psalm 133:1-3, *In agreement, the Lord commands the blessing to the high and the low alike.*

Power Key: *Agreement Is The Requirement For Answered Prayer.*

The relationship between a husband and wife is more than a love affair between the two. It is God's source for miracles within the home. *1 Peter 3:7-9, In the same way you married men should live considerately with [your wives], with an intelligent recognition [of the marriage relation], honoring the woman as [physically] the weaker, but [realizing that you] are joint heirs of the grace (God's unmerited favor) of life, in order that your prayers may not be hindered and cutoff. [Otherwise you cannot pray effectively.] Finally, all [of you] should be of one and the same mind (united in spirit), sympathizing [with one another], loving [each other] as brethren [of one household], compassionate and courteous (tender-hearted and humble).* For a man to live *considerately* with his wife means, he should consider his wife's opinions and ideas. Agreement is never tyranny nor chauvinism; it is humanity and kindness.

Most Christians are too quick to throw the cliché, "Agree to disagree," into friendship and marriage. The sixty-four dollar question then is, "With whom does one agree?" When a husband, wife and children are together, the obvious one with whom to agree is the head – the father. When the father is not present, the children must agree with the mother. In a church setting, the body must never agree with a deacon board over the pastor.

Do not the arms, legs and feet agree with the signals sent from the brain without debate? A carpenter who bangs his thumb with his own hammer has experienced the involuntary reaction of self-inflicted pain. Or is it involuntary? The brain sends a signal to the thumb saying, "Get out of the way, here comes the hammer!" The thumb, then, has ample time to move, but if it is not in complete and absolute agreement with the rest of the body, or the eyes become distracted; it gets smashed. ***Agreement follows protocol and always yields to the head first and follows succinctly.*** When a pastor is in another man of God's church, he is required to submit and acquiesce to the headship of the pastor or evangelist in question. The proper etiquette for a man of God is depicted in I Corinthians 14:32, *For the spirits of the prophets (the speakers in tongues) are under the speaker's control [and subject to being silenced as may be necessary].*

Ezekiel 11:17-20 (KJV), Therefore say, thus saith the Lord God; I will even gather you from the people, and assemble you out of the countries where ye have been scattered, and I will give you the land of Israel. And they shall come thither, and they shall take away all the detestable things thereof and all the abominations thereof from thence. And I will give them one heart, and I will put a new spirit within you; and I will take the stony, and will give them an heart of flesh: that they may walk in my statutes, and keep mine ordinances, and do them: and

they shall be My people and I will be their God.

God's strategy for your success is to first position you for agreement, then wash you with the Word, and give you a heart transplant. Without this heart transplant, you cannot function and flow in the spirit of agreement.

There are many people who try to flow in agreement, but they are still functioning with a heart of stone. Their heart is full of unforgiveness and bitterness. You will never be able to agree totally with your husband, your pastor or your superior if you are harboring unforgiveness. You must first release and forgive every offense in your life. Then, God will make agreeing virtually effortless. The heart He places in you is the same heart He gives each believer. The word *one* as used in *"And I will give them one heart..."* gets its meaning from the Hebrew word, *'echad* which means unified, united, first, alike, altogether. It is the heart of agreement. It is a heart throbbing with the desire for its Creator.

Power Key: *The Heart Of Agreement Is The Heartbeat Of God.*

When an individual does not serve and agree with his superiors with a heart of humility, he is functioning under the principle of *obligatory agreement.* Whether it is a father, mother, husband, pastor, or boss, if you are simply in agreement with them out of obligation, you are wasting your time.

If obligatory agreement is not the kind of agreement you should walk in what kind of agreement does God expect from His people? Godly agreement calls for Blood Covenant. Covenant agreement deals with the spirit, while obligatory agreement deals with flesh.

The Apostle Paul encourages the believer, in the twelfth chapter of Romans, to live peaceably with all men. This is not calling for agreement, rather it gives a directive to find the agreeable factor and concede to one another. There are matters of great importance that God intends for believers to agree upon. Nevertheless, because of the believer's inability to live peaceably with one another on simple terms, no one enjoys the bigger picture.

How thoughtless, the reactions of grown men and women when they cannot agree on what to eat, where to go, or who goes first. These matters are of inconsequential value, because they are earthly. The only thing that matters is the supernatural. In light of this understanding, God's people should strive to keep relationships open, free from offense, so that He may give direction in carrying out His desires. I need you and you need me; we need each other. Remember the passage at the beginning, how can two walk together unless they agree?

Power Key: *It Was Agreement Before It Was Love.*

When Adam and Eve walked in the Garden of Eden, they flowed in total agreement one with another. Their relationship was not founded on their ability to "fall in love", because falling in love was not yet an available source for happiness. Society, today, believes falling in love is based more on what one can see. Adam and Eve's love was agreement. Their love was dictated by a higher standard set by the upper echelons of Heaven.

Genesis 1:26, God said, let Us [Father, Son and Holy Spirit] make mankind in Our image, after Our likeness, and let them have complete authority over the fish of the sea, the birds of the air, the [tame] beasts, and over all of the earth, and over everything that creeps upon the earth. God refers to Adam as plural, "them" and "they".

God looked at man and saw that he was alone. Every creature that God created had its counterpart, except for Adam. The Scriptures do not imply that Adam was lonely, rather, that he was alone. God was empathic with man's feelings, because He had been alone Himself until he created Adam. Everything God desires for Himself, He wants for mankind as well.

God did not take a new clump of clay and design a woman for man, instead, when God wanted a new thing, He made it come out of something He had already made. Thusly, it was sustained by whatever He took it from. *Proverbs 16:4a, The Lord has made everything to accommodate itself and contribute to its own end and His own purpose.* Everything congruently works together through agreement, just as woman was already resident within man. Everything God wants to give you is already within your grasp awaiting your recognition.

Adam and Eve had everything they needed in the garden, but they wanted something they could not have. Their selfish desires caused God to turn their perfect agreement into conditional love. In Genesis 3:16b, the Bible states, *"Yet your **desire** and craving will be for your husband, and he will **rule** over you."* The literal translation of the word *"desire"* means to run over. God caused the love between man and woman to become tainted with competitiveness over who would rule. God made Adam to rule over the woman. The word *"rule"* means, to have dominion, governor, superiority in mental action. Thus, the perfect, equal union between man and woman became hostile and competitive.

~The Apex Of Relationships~

Marriage is the apex of relationships known to man, because it requires a lifetime commitment. This is the highest level of agreement any two people can share on the earth. God's exclusivity for marriage is based on the **Blood Covenant** that takes place between a man and wife, and happens to no other two. The Bible states that the "two become one flesh" not one spirit. The relationship between a husband and wife is a spiritual concession and a natural merger. When a woman leaves her home and a man leaves his father and mother, the two become one. I am continually amazed with God's mathematical system. It is staggering how God can take two and make one, while at other times, he adds one to one and puts to flight a host of ten thousand. Furthermore, when a woman comes into agreement with her husband, an even greater mystery occurs. Perhaps, the union between a husband and wife has a greater intensity than just two ordinary people coming together. *Deuteronomy 32:30, How should one chase a thousand, and two put ten thousand to flight...?*

~The Law And Anointing Of Agreement~

The law of agreement works in accordance with the agreement between two people and the anointing of agreement works with "the principle of the third". The principle of the third is the synergistic effort of any three entities resulting in magnified strength. Two people coming together in the name of Jesus are operating in the principle of the third, by virtue of the Holy Spirit. As stated in Ecclesiastes 4:12b, *"a three-fold cord is not easily broken."*

When a woman cleaves unto her husband, there is a far more superior effect than the same man with his mother, because the Holy Spirit is the unifier. Stormie Omartian writes in her book, The Power of A Praying Wife, *"A wife's prayers for her husband have even a far greater affect on him than his mother's. A mother's prayers for her children are fervent. When a man marries, he leaves his father and mother and becomes one with his wife. They are a team, one unit, unified in spirit. The strength of a husband and wife in God's sight is far greater than the sum of the strength of the two individuals. That is because the Holy Spirit unites them and gives them added power to their prayers."*

A love that is built on the bedrock of agreement, and not on emotion, will never lack for desire. Couples, whose marriages are on the rocks, need to understand the force of agreement and persevere past the storm. There is a supernatural love rooted in the foundation of time itself just around the bend.

Marriage is like a drive through the Rockies in

Colorado. You may be driving through the valleys of life with boulders on either side. If you will hold on to your original agreement, a beautiful panoramic view will soon spread before you. There, you can run, skip, and frolic with the one you agreed to love for life.

The amount of energy, time, money and emotion that it takes to salvage and rescue a dying relationship is not as involved as beginning a brand new one. What happens when a husband or a wife decides he or she cannot live with their spouse? They may walk away and live through the nightmare of divorce. On the other hand, they may begin with someone new with no promise of improvement the second time around. The energy expended to figure out what the new lover likes, loves, hates, wants, can live with, cannot live without is far more demanding. In a marriage of even two years, the parties have already learned, if nothing else, what the other does not like. Selfishness often wins out when the parties refuse to invest time in doing what their partner *does* like. Still, agreement faddishly makes the bold statement and shouts, "WHATEVER!" The agreeable factor does not always come neatly wrapped in gold foil and fancy bows. There are times when the response may arrive in a wrinkled, old, half-torn paper bag and the power of agreement still produces the unexpected. Do not walk in offense, because of an old sack; use it to carry away the fruit of your agreement - Favor!

~God's View On Divorce~

Perhaps, God's hatred towards divorce is understandable when viewed from the vantage of covenant agreement. We are talking about more than "irreconcilable differences"; it is about covenant breaking. I am not implying that God does not forgive divorce; I believe that He is a loving and forgiving God. Nevertheless, He abhors divorce. *Malachi 2:13-15, And this you do with double guilt; you cover the altar of the Lord with tears [shed by your unoffending wives, divorced by you that you might take heathen wives], and with [your own] weeping and crying out because the Lord does not regard your offering any more or accept it with favor at your hand. Yet you ask, why does he reject it? Because the Lord was witness [to the covenant made at your marriage] between you and the wife of your youth, against whom you have dealt treacherously and to whom you were faithless. Yet she is your companion and the wife of your covenant [made by your marriage vows]. And did not God make [you and your wife] one [flesh]? Did not One make you and preserve your spirit alive? And why [did God make you two] one? Because He sought a godly offspring [from your union] therefore take heed to yourselves, and let no one deal treacherously and be faithless to the wife of his youth. For the Lord, the God of Israel, says: I hate divorce and marital separation and him who covers his garment [his wife] with violence. Therefore keep a watch upon your spirit [that it may be controlled by my Spirit], that you deal not treacherously and faithlessly [with your marriage mate].* Wow, that needs neither explanation nor expounding; the Word speaks for itself! ***God is into this covenant agreement "thing" a whole lot more than Christians realize.***

Power Key: *Forgiveness Is The Foundation For Rebuilding.*

What are the options for a failing marriage? From a worldly view, divorce tops the charts. From God's view, forgiveness is at the top and commitment to the covenant of marriage.

God designed relationships based on His own relationship with man. Man was the prototype and the maximization of what He created. Therefore, marriage is the maximization of earthly relationships. He made man in His own image and man became the recipient of His love.

Power Key: *Intimacy Holds The Power Of Creation.*

I Peter 3:6a, It was thus that Sarah obeyed Abraham [following his guidance and acknowledging his headship over her by] calling him lord (master, leader, authority). Abraham and Sarah's relationship is noteworthy, in that their love affair with life began at the ripe old age of 100. Can you imagine waiting to get excited about life until your latter years?

Power Key: *A Relationship Is Never Hopeless When Agreement Is Present.*

Abraham's purpose became known when God made His agreement with him. Obviously, he could not carry out the obligation of the agreement by himself. He needed his counterpart, Sarah. At first, Sarah tried to avert her assignment in the agreement and gave Abraham her handmaiden, Hagar. Perhaps, she felt incompetent at her age carrying out such a ridiculous task. It is not known for sure. Nevertheless, she failed the agreement and Ishmael was born.

Power Key: *Agreement Is Your Exit From Adversity.*

God sent a messenger angel to Abraham and Sarah to get them back on track. He reassured them that He would keep His end of the bargain if they would by faith keep theirs. Every relationship will, at some point or another, go off track, but the original covenant agreement made between two people is always God's original and intended purpose. *Genesis 17:1-2, When Abram was ninety-nine years old, the Lord appeared to him and said, I Am the Almighty God; walk and live habitually before Me and be perfect (blameless, wholehearted, complete). And I will make My covenant (solemn pledge) between Me and you and will multiply you exceedingly.* Within twelve months, the promise of God's agreement with Abraham was fulfilled and Isaac was born. Oh, how Abraham and Sarah laughed with joy as they beheld the fulfillment of what God had promised them.

Prayer of Agreement:

Dear Lord, Thank You for the relationships You have brought into my life. I thank You that they are divine connections. Strengthen me and help me to be a right person in someone's life today.

Amen

Power Keys:

~Relationships Were Made For Agreement.
~Agreement Looks Beyond What Is and Sees What Will Be.
~Agreement Is The Binding Force To Any Successful Relationship.
~Agreement Is The Requirement For Answered Prayer.
~The Heart Of Agreement Is The Heartbeat Of God.
~It Was Agreement Before It Was Love.
~Forgiveness Is The Foundation For Rebuilding.
~Intimacy Holds The Power Of Creation.
~A Relationship Is Never Hopeless When Agreement Is Present.
~Agreement Is Your Exit From Adversity.

~17~

THE PARADE OF LIFE

Power Key: *The Performance Of Life Plays Out Whether The Players Know It Or Not.*

The fulfillment of each promise for every agreement will always override the difficulty of the journey. I heard a story, the other day, based on the musical called The Parade. It is the account of a dedicated, hardworking Jewish man whose commitment to his employer puts him at the wrong place at the wrong time.

It is the morning of Memorial Day. The setting is in the Deep South somewhere in Georgia in the early 1900's. While the majority of the small, southern town is out watching the Memorial Day parade, one of the young girls who works at the factory enters the office of the diligent employee. She goes there seeking to be paid for her time. The man asks for her employee number, hands her the check and sends her on her way.

This man has only been married a couple of years and yet, his relationship with his wife is somewhat dry and lifeless. At the end of a long laborious day, he finds his way back home. His faithful wife is waiting for some form of romance or desire. They go to sleep. Meanwhile, sometime during the night, someone murders the innocent young girl, sadly known by her employee number only.

Early the next morning, there is a knock at the door; it is the sheriff and deputy. They begin to question him and they carry him down to the station. With no defense or alibi, he is quickly arrested and thrown in jail. No one could prove his innocence; he could only rely on his good character and moral work ethics he so carefully guarded. Assured of his innocence and good character, he impatiently awaits his obvious acquittal. His wife of two years comes to visit each day with fresh food. He is somewhat aloof and coolly kisses her, all the while, there appears to be no chemistry between them.

The story continues and he is brought before a judge, who is easily bought, and a jury full of hatred. He still has no defense and no one in the prejudiced neighborhood dares step forward in his defense. The trial begins and, within three days, he is pronounced guilty! His wife remains hopeful and willing to fight for her husband's fate. His frustration and pain, from being wrongfully accused, only adds to his frigid demeanor. He attempts to handle the situation alone and begins to study law books hoping to stand in his own defense before an appellate court. She sings a song about him doing it alone. He is unable to recognize the power in his own Jewish faith. A Jewish ceremony is all about covenant. She is bound to her husband by oath and not by emotion.

Exasperated by the injustice, she decides to do what she can. She makes an appeal to the Governor and he schedules her husband's appearance before the courts, once again, to prove his innocence. His eyes are unveiled to the blessing of the covenant of matrimony. He sings a song of recognition to his wife sharing his intimate feelings of gratitude and love. In the meantime, he is transferred to a new facility. His patient wife makes the trip to the new prison and bribes the warden for a conjugal visit with her husband. Clad with picnic basket, blankets, and much love, she spends a perfect day with her husband. He says to his wife, "I hope you will be able to bribe the warden again, so we can share more moments like today." She bids her husband farewell and offers these words of hope, "There won't be any need to bribe the warden and soon you'll be home with me."

It is the eve of Memorial Day. The annual parade is scheduled to march through town as usual while a man who has been wrongfully accused lays in his prison cell content and ever grateful for the blessing of his partner. What a way to end a beautiful love story. Except, it does not end there.

On this same night of contentment and joy a band of officers from the sheriff's department come and whisk the innocent man away. He pleads for mercy, yet, finds none. Let us not forget, once before in another time and another place, an innocent Jew was cruelly and unjustly murdered.

The scenery on the stage during the musical is simply a lonely, old oak tree. The bloodthirsty men try the Jew on the spot; they convict him and hang him until he dies. When the sun comes up everyone is once again gathered at the town square for the annual Memorial Day parade. It has been one full year since the beginning of one man's nightmare. And the parade marches on.

An innocent girl is murdered and the parade of life marches on...

An innocent man is murdered and the parade of life marches on...

A faithful wife is left a widow and the parade of life marches on...

Yet, in her finest hour; in the briefness of one chapter of her life, she rescues her husband from a greater evil than death itself. And the parade of life marches on...

The faithfulness of her agreement snatched him from the wicked hands of *lifeless-life*. And a man, once dead, lived one day full of peace, hope, and love, because his wife refused to come out of her *Agreement.*

And the parade of life marches on...

Power Key: *Better To Live One Day In The Shadow Of Agreement, Than To Live A Lifetime With The Death From Offense.*

The understanding of covenant agreement is the beginning of life. Do not allow the parade of life to march on without you. Can you see the God of Covenant Agreement? He is present; He is there with you. Right where you are.

Genesis 18:1-3, Now the Lord appeared to

Abraham by the oaks or terebinths of Mamre; as he sat at the door of his tent in the heat of the day, he lifted up his eyes and looked, and behold, three men stood at a little distance from him. He ran from the tent door to meet them and bowed himself to the ground and said, my Lord, if now I have found favor in your sight, do not pass by your servant, I beg of you. Perhaps, these three men whom Abraham called Lord were the three agreed parties of the Godhead. It is evident that God would not need any help from angels to speak His will. The only question here is do angels have the power to execute judgment upon the earth? The trek of two of the beings is followed right into the wiles and wickedness of Sodom and Gomorrah where they destroy the two cities within the course of 24 hours.

Meanwhile, Abraham's covenant agreement with God provided a protection from judgment. It flowed into his offspring, Isaac, and even the men of his household including his servants. When a man walks in agreement with God's purpose for his life, everyone in his household is protected under the agreement.

Power Key: ***The Fulfillment Of Agreement Is The Promise.***

As with Abraham and Hagar's connection, you must guard your relationships from producing Ishmaels. These are the illegitimate sons of relationship which dilute and scatter the fruit of your favor.

~*Prison Praise*~

Every relationship belongs in your past, in your present or your future. Paul and Timothy celebrated a prosperous, divine connection. Timothy, Paul's protégé, remained in agreement with Paul and their relationship gave birth to the church at Ephesus. Another relationship from Paul's past was with a man named Barnabas. Barnabas came out of agreement with Paul, because of a dispute over Barnabas' nephew. Barnabas insisted on carrying his nephew, John Mark, into their future. Therefore, Paul and Barnabas parted ways and Barnabas came into agreement with John Mark and was never heard of again. Later, John Mark proved himself and afterward reconnected with Paul and penned the most detailed account of the Gospel, the book of Mark.

When Silas came into Paul's life, it was a divine designation of time. He came at the appropriate hour and stood in agreement with Paul during a difficult time in his life. *Acts 16:23-26, And when they had struck them with many blows, they threw them into prison, charging the jailer to keep them safely. He, having received [so strict a] charge, put them into the inner prison (the dungeon) and fastened their feet in the stocks. But about midnight, as Paul and Silas were praying and singing hymns of praise to God, and the [other] prisoners were listening to them, suddenly there was a great earthquake, so that the very foundations of the prison were shaken; and at once all the doors were opened and everyone's shackles were unfastened.* The agreement between Paul and Silas released a fragrant worship, so powerful and so potent, that the earth shook. Every shackle in the prison, including all the doors, were subject to the anointing of agreement.

Power Key: *The Fragrance Of Agreement Is Worship.*

This is a moment in time when the natural laws of physics must yield to the maker of every molecule that holds solid matter together. The prison doors could not maintain their present status in the presence of pure, undefiled worship.

~*The Sons Of Thunder*~

Mark 10:35, And James and John, the sons of Zebedee, approached Him and said to Him, Teacher, we desire You to do for us whatever we ask of You. And He replied to them, What do you desire Me to do for you? And they said to Him, grant that we may sit, one at Your right hand and one at [Your] left hand, in Your glory (Your majesty and splendor). But Jesus said to them, you do not know what you are asking. Are you able to drink the cup that I drink or be baptized with the baptism [of affliction] with which I am baptized? And they replied, we are able. And Jesus told them, the cup that I drink you will drink, and you will be baptized with the baptism with which I am baptized, but to sit at My right hand or My left hand is not Mine to give; but [it will be given to those] for whom it is ordained and prepared.

Most people look upon this scene as audacious and immature. What could these two sons of Zebedee be thinking? I believe, because these two brothers were in such agreement; they had reached another level in the Spirit where almost anything is possible. They approached Jesus with a confidence and assurance that He could do whatever they asked. They wanted the reinforcement of the third person.

Matthew 20:20-24, Then the mother of Zebedee's children came up to Him with her sons and, kneeling worshiped Him and asked a favor of Him. And He asked her, what do you wish? She answered Him, give orders that these two sons of mine may sit, one at Your right hand and one at your left in Your kingdom. But Jesus replied, you do not realize what you are asking. Are you able to drink the cup that I am about to drink and to be baptized with the baptism with which I am baptized? They answered, we are able. He said to them, you will drink My cup but seats at My right hand and left are not Mine to give, but they are for those for whom they have been ordained and prepared by my Father. But when the ten [other disciples] heard this, they were indignant at the two brothers. The two boys, along with their mother, bowed themselves in worship at Jesus feet disproving the theory they were seeking selfish honor. The other disciples were offended at what these two were asking. The words Jesus shares gives the appearance Jesus was rebuking the boys. Quite the contrary, Jesus was rebuking the other disciples who were entertaining feelings of jealousy, envy and offense. *Verse 26-28, Not so shall it be among you; but whoever wishes to be great among you must be your servant, and whoever desires to be first among you must be your slave. Just as the Son of Man*

came not to be waited on but to serve, and to give His life as a ransom for many [the price paid to set them free]. The two Zebedee boys came not with an arrogant attitude, rather, with the posture of humility. They bowed down on their knees before Christ and in essence were asking to be given the privilege of serving at the right and left hand of Jesus. They, who were willing to leave everything including family, demonstrated their deep devotion and love for Christ. Would you not want your children to find their place on either side of the One who saved them?

These young boys, overzealous as they might have appeared, had tapped into a realm of faith that went above and beyond the power of one person's faith. Perhaps, we judge the zeal of young believers too quickly. Their attack, on wanting the impossible, was a result of more than youthfulness. Once again, the power of supernatural exponential dynamics revealed a deeper and greater level of anointing. Jesus said, "Greater works than these shall ye do."

Am I saying these two boys ever had a chance at attaining the two seats on either side of God's throne? Absolutely not, that would be absurd. I am saying they had a different level of faith that was unlocked by their willingness to agree with one another. They dared to go on a journey beyond faith. Where else could they get the boldness to broach such a bequest? The word "able" used in their response, when Jesus asked if they were able to drink of His cup, means ability, strength, miracle power, a mighty wonderful work. It is derived from the Greek word *dunamai*, which is cousin to the word *dunamis*, meaning dynamite power.

Most Christians may never tap into a level of faith as such. The absence of humility and the presence of disagreement result in neutrality that disables the church. Do you agree; it is time to arm oneself with the weapons of humility, agreement and worship? Think of the boundless, innumerable blessings God's people are missing, because of our ineptness with relationships. Your inability to get along with someone near you is costing you greatly.

Power Key: *Humility And Worship Are The Keys To Boundless Blessings Hidden In Agreement.*

Only the humble and the true worshipper can access the keys. These boys were not your common neighborhood rebels; they were in submission to their father before they enlisted with Jesus. Their eagerness in walking the walk with Jesus may strike you as extreme. Yet, I believe this is the kind of obedience that unlocks the "greater works" referred to by Jesus. Agreement with the right people will afford you the ability to do greater works than the Apostles and Jesus ever did!

What kind of relationships are you nurturing?

Are they "good" relationships or God-relationships? Do they produce good fruit?

Prayer of Agreement:

Dear Lord, Thank You for the relationships You have brought into my life. I thank You that they are divine

connections. Strengthen me and help me to be a right person in someone's life today.

Amen

Power Keys:

~The Performance Of Life Plays Out Whether The Players Know It Or Not.
~Better To Live One Day In The Shadow Of Agreement, Than To Live A Lifetime With The Death Of Offense.
~The Fulfillment Of Agreement Is The Promise.
~The Fragrance Of Agreement Is Worship.
~Humility And Worship Are The Keys To Boundless Blessings Hidden In Agreement.

~18~

THE ANOINTING OF AGREEMENT

Power Key: *The Anointing Of Agreement Is The Most Powerful Force In The Universe By Its Very Nature.*

 ehold, how good and how pleasant it is for brethren to dwell together in unity! It is like the precious ointment poured on the head, that ran down the beard, even the beard of Aaron [the first High Priest], that came down the collar and skirts of his garments [consecrating the whole body]. It is like the dew of [lofty] Mount Hermon and the dew that comes on the hills of Zion; for there the Lord has commanded the blessing, even life forevermore [upon the high and the lowly] (Psalm 133:1-3). The oil, that ran down this first High Priest's beard, is the very anointing I write about with much humility and fear, within this chapter. This anointing will break the yoke of offense in believers everywhere. *I am fully persuaded the Anointing of Agreement will ultimately usher in the second coming of Christ.*

All my life, I have viewed the Scriptures from a simple, naïve mindset; I am convinced everything the Bible says is true. I believe very strongly, that the accounts in the Scriptures all happened. I have no problem believing the Red Sea was split in half, that Jesus walked on the water, that He defied the law of physics and walked through walls. My faith has always been way out there. When I began teaching on the Power of Agreement, my eyes were enlightened to the power of the principle that all things work in congruent effort creating what we know as the three-dimensional world. That is the law of agreement. I mentioned, in Chapter Six, how a light bulb works together with electricity to produce light. Electricity is useless without the light bulb as the bulb is useless without electricity. That may sound like simple math, one plus one equals two. Yet, subtraction becomes the mathematical operation most Christians choose. I have been praying for the past 13 years asking the Lord to move supernaturally within the Body of Christ.

~The Seed Of Agreement~

On June 28, 2000, I celebrated the one-year anniversary of the first time I taught on the Power of Agreement. Ironically, it was one year after God commanded Abraham to walk in the agreement He had made with Him, that Isaac, the son of promise was born. I remember asking the members of my congregation at Power Church to sow a seed of agreement. We all agreed not to come out of the agreement for a supernatural harvest on our seeds.

Allow me to go back and fill in the story in greater detail.

~Satan's Last Ditch Effort To Stop The Agreement~

December of 1999, a few days before Christmas, I was struck by a strange malady with the most intense pain I have ever felt. It was an attack on the right cheek of my face that almost immobilized me. I withstood the pain long enough to make it through our New Year's Eve celebration. I was now moving into the third week of this sickness. I finally made an appointment and sought the advice of my doctor thinking it was a deeply impacted sinus problem. X-rays were ordered with no signs of any sinus problems. I made an appointment with my dentist being almost certain that it was an abscessed tooth. Again X-rays were taken and my whole mouth was numbed with anesthetics with no relief from the fierce pain. I was then directed to an ear, nose and throat specialist who examined me and directed me to, yet another specialist, a neurologist. Meanwhile, I was in such pain and there was no painkiller available to cut the intensity, even a small percentage. Unable to sleep, I began to cry out to God, all the while thinking, this must be a last ditch effort to keep me from moving into the new millennium with the intensity I had already purposed in my heart.

The doctor reached a verdict on this medical mystery, and diagnosed the problem as trigeminal neuralgia.

This is a rare condition known as the most excruciating pain man can endure. It attacks the trigeminal nerve on the face with an electrical shock-like pain. By the second day of the new millennium, it was obvious that this attack was solely to keep me from engaging in the events of January 2nd.

~Uncommon Worship~

January 2, 2000, I awoke from what little sleep I was able to steal away. My wife urged me and practically forbade me from pressing on to preach that morning. She had already called my assistant pastor who agreed to fill my pulpit. I refused to allow my ailments to keep me from worshipping the Lord. Knowing I was no master at pain management I figured I would lead the worship and praise service, hide behind my keyboards, and leave the preaching to the assistant.

~Crazy Praise~

I remember thinking how crazy the last month had gone. I had finished out the last part of the 20th century in crutches (That's a whole other story). There I was, the big faith preacher; I had just gotten off crutches and now I was struggling to open my mouth. I sat at the keyboards and began to play; thank God for the anointing that began to break through the pain. I struggled to move my lips the pain had an almost numbing effect. We sang the old

song, "Going to the Chapel"; I had rewritten the words
and it always evokes great joy and happiness in our congregation, something I was not feeling at the moment.

Could this be the day,
The sky's so very blue.
Birds are singing as if they knew.
Today's the day when Jesus comes again,
And we'll never be lonely anymore.
Because we're going to heaven
And we're gonna see Jesus...

I was trying to put on the garments of praise for the
spirit of heaviness, when all of a sudden I heard the Holy
Spirit say, *"Worship and praise me like you've never
done before."* I got up from the keyboards and declared
the Word of the Lord. I worshipped and began to preach
and prophesy. It was the birthplace of what I call "Crazy
Praise."

~Debt For Debt~

"Crazy Praise" is based on the seemingly insane
instruction to send praisers first during a battle. It is
obvious, if you are trying to win a battle, you do not send
the band in first; you send the troops first and then, the
band celebrates the victory. People began to dance, run,
jump and praise the Lord like I have never seen before. I
mentioned earlier that God had instructed us to receive an
offering. This was no ordinary offering. Crazy as it may
sound, God instructed everyone who had credit card debt
to sow a sizeable seed on their credit cards. God asked,
"What do you think could happen if my people were will-

ing to go into debt for My kingdom as easily as they are for gifts around the holidays?" I shared with the congregation what God had asked and people began to line up to charge a seed on their credit cards. It seems absolutely crazy to increase your debt to get out of debt. I sowed a seed that maxed-out one of my credit cards. At this point, I was willing to do anything to get some relief from the pain I was in. We continued in crazy praise for the remainder of the service and the excitement only grew as the afternoon wore on. That same evening, I was out with my family after service; we had dinner and the pain in my face had subsided greatly.

~Recognition Of The Psalmist Anointing~

January 9, 2000 Apostle Louis Greenup, known as the marriage doctor, was scheduled to speak. He has ministered on the average of two times per year for the past seven years in my church. His focus has always been on marriage ministry. This time Apostle Louis came into recognition of the anointing of worship upon my life. He was moved by the music and began to prophesy. The Prophet had summoned a minstrel that released an anointing unlike he had ever experienced. He spoke of the things the Holy Spirit was about to do in my life. He said God was grooming me for a global assignment. He spoke of television ministries and stadiums filled with tens of thousands of people worshipping. He spoke in detail of the entourage of people that would accompany my travels and even the lawyers to protect the ministry. It was a detailed prophecy unlike I had ever heard.

Prophetess Juanita Bynum, a dear friend of mine, had also prophesied that I would be ministering to stadiums filled with people a couple of years prior. Here came the confirmation.

~*Worship Marathon*~

February 13, 2000, Power Church celebrated its 12th anniversary. God had instructed us all to dress in white. My precious friend, Tammy Faye (Bakker) Messner, was our guest speaker; she brought a stirring word for the Body to walk in forgiveness. We would discover the symbolism of wearing white in a vision my mother had a couple of months later.

Sunday, June 25th one of my nieces was scheduled to be married. I officiated the wedding at 4:00 pm and received an instruction from the Holy Spirit to begin a 72-hour worship marathon. Jesus' first miracle was at the wedding of Cana. The evening worship service released a prophetic anointing over me. The worship was powerful with many of the wedding guests still present. A heavy mantle of unity and agreement filled the sanctuary and I boldly commanded each person to flow in unity with the Holy Spirit. Surprisingly, as far as I could tell there was absolute agreement. Everyone spoke in tongues. At the end of the service, I followed through with the instruction from the Lord and began the worship marathon. I did not leave the church for the next four days. Members of the congregation came in shifts of four hour increments each day and a holy worship was offered up to God nonstop.

~God Gives The Seed Its Assignment~

Tuesday morning about 2:00 AM, I was sitting in my office with a few people when it dawned on me that it was June 28. It had been one year since the Lord had revealed the Law of Agreement. The following day, during the Wednesday service, I understood the difference between the Law of Agreement and the Anointing of Agreement for the first time. Once again, we sowed. Each member came forward with their seed and shook my hand in agreement. I had shared the principle of sowing the seed on the wings of worship and it was understood the seed of agreement would receive its assignment from God. We went away anticipating the unexpected. The unimaginable! God spoke to me again and said, "How would you like to delve into what another 24 hours of worship could do?" I jubilantly yielded to the call and we carried the worship through to the next day. By this time I was feeling the deprivation of sleep, still, I remember pressing on until 4:00 AM that morning. I was mindful to keep the worship flowing and secured someone to carry the torch while I slept for an hour or two.

~God Releases The Anointing Of Agreement~

On Thursday, June 28th, while sitting at my desk, I commented to my two assistants of the sweet ambiance in my office. I realized the agreement mingled with worship was creating an atmosphere of total peace. It was like an ecosphere where everything was sustained by the connectivity and function of one thing to the other. I went into the sanctuary to worship and met up with my mother who had just completed her four hours of worship. She had been crying and began to recount a vision she had experienced while worshipping.

She said, *"I was on my face before the Lord, and I was crying. When I arose, I was unable to walk, because the anointing was heavy upon me. I felt as though I were intoxicated and fell back on my face. I continued in worship and I saw the Lord sitting on a majestic throne. He sat on the east side listening to my son's music. There was a great multitude of people dressed in white robes with the appearance of angels. They stood before my son as he directed their music with a director's baton. The Spirit spoke and said, 'They are not angels; it is the Bride of Christ.' The sea of people marched in unity towards the throne and I heard, in the background, the song my son had recently written. It is a triumphant melody entitled, Song of the Bride."* I kissed my mother's cheek and returned with great emotion to my office. Three of my staff members met me there and I began to recount the beautiful vision with tears in my eyes. I was so stirred I could not remember the details, so I summoned my sister who was present when my mother shared the vision. We stood around my desk reveling in the glory of the moment. My graphic artist came to the door with a proof copy of my new teaching tape series. I could sense his apprehension upon entering the room. He had walked into a heavy anointing unexpectedly. I looked over the artwork as my sister, Elizabeth, fearfully spoke of a heavy anointing she could feel emanating from the adjoining wall between my office and the sanctuary. At that very moment, the Spirit of the Lord moved upon the people who were present and seized everyone of us. We, involuntarily and simultaneously, fell prostrate before the Lord and began to weep. A few minutes passed by and I felt an urgency which propelled me into the sanctuary where I immediately buckled under the anointing and fell to the floor at the back of the auditorium. I tried to get up to move toward the altar, but was unable. I struggled and managed a crawl when my sister entered behind me. I motioned her to come to me and I gave her the instruction from the Lord. He had instructed me to empty every office and usher everyone within the building into the sanctuary. He said He was about to move in a mighty way.

~The Unimaginable!~

My sister quickly ran and I made my way to the altar. Everyone in the building, including two children, met at the altar. We all lay prostrate in a circle with our heads toward the center. We linked arms, much like a team of skydivers carefully preparing the execution of a daring stunt. I could sense the presence of God pressing in upon us. I felt as though we were falling, yet, felt the support of a wind undergirding us. Without prompting, several of us began to scream and cry as the fury of God's presence passed over. I then, saw a globe and God poured out an anointing that enveloped it from top to bottom. God had deposited the Anointing of Agreement. Each person present gave a similar account of the experience.

Jesus said, *"Greater works than these shall ye do."* What Peter could not do in three years of ministry with Jesus, he did in one day under the Anointing of Agreement. The power behind His ministry, that day, came from their upper room experience with the Holy Spirit who was released because of their agreement.

What the Church was unable to do in 2000 years, God's Covenant people motivated by the anointing of agreement will perform! *"Eye hath not seen, nor ear heard, nor have entered into the heart of man the things…"*

The unimaginable!

PRAYER OF AGREEMENT:

Dear Lord Jesus, I ask You to baptize me with Your precious Spirit. Fill me with Your Anointing of Agreement: the agreement between You, the Father, the Son, and the Holy Ghost. I want to be one with You. Help me to be quick in my obedience to Your commands.
Amen

POWER KEY:

~The Anointing Of Agreement Is The Most Powerful Force In The Universe By Its Very Nature.

~19~

JOURNEY BEYOND FAITH

Power Key: *The Marriage Of Faith And Agreement Produces The Unimaginable.*

*ut solid food is for full grown men, for those whose **senses** and **mental faculties** are trained by practice to discriminate and distinguish between what is morally good and noble and what is evil and contrary either to divine or human law. Therefore let us go on and get past the elementary stage in the teachings and doctrine of Christ (the Messiah), advancing steadily toward the completeness and perfection that belong to spiritual maturity. Let us not again be laying the foundation of repentance and abandonment of dead works (dead formalism) and of the faith [by which you turned] to God, With teachings about purifying, the lay-*

ing on of hands, the resurrection from the dead, and eternal judgment and punishment. [These are all matters of which you should have been fully aware long, long ago.] If indeed God permits, we will [now] proceed [to advanced teaching]. For it is impossible [to restore and bring again to repentance] those who have been once for all enlightened, who have consciously tasted the heavenly gift and have become sharers of the Holy Spirit, And have felt how good the Word of god is and the mighty powers of the age and world to come. If they then deviate from the faith and turn away from their allegiance-[it is impossible] to bring them back to repentance, for (because, while, as long as) they nail upon the cross the Son of God afresh [as far as they are concerned] and are holding [Him] up to contempt and shame and public disgrace. (Hebrews 5:14-6:1-6)

The fathers of faith mentioned, in Chapter Eleven in the Book of Hebrews, were men of faith who were looking for a city whose architect is God. They were utilizing their faith for more than acquiring and amassing things in the natural. They had a deeper desire for relationship with their Creator. They received God's approval, because of their faith. ***These great martyrs of faith went beyond what they believed and entered into a realm where faith was no longer the act of believing rather; it was sheer obedience.***

There are times when your faith will take on the character of obedience and agreement. God told Abraham to journey to a land he had never seen before. By faith, by agreeing to God's instruction, Abraham set out to find this land.

Most believers have known faith simply as a method for producing "things." These are things they have seen with their eyes, but maybe have never had before. Faith is not faith until you believe for something you have never seen. To believe (or have faith) for a car is not faith, because you can see a car. Faith is the substance of things hoped for the evidence of things *"not seen"*. *To Journey Beyond your Faith is the agreement between the Word, your intellect and your spirit.* It is a place where your faith matures to the level of believing for truly the impossible. In the opening text, the writer is setting the stage for going beyond faith.

There is a realm in the Spirit where one goes beyond faith into the Presence of God and faith is no longer the basis for sustenance. It is a place where His Presence and the knowledge of His Word become so evident you do not require faith. It is like unzipping a porthole from this dimension to another dimension where everything "unseen" is seen.

At some point or another, every believer's faith will fail him or her. I have experienced the pain of not being able to stir up faith to support what I have become convinced in my mind was the truth according to God's Word. Have you ever believed something in your head, but found it difficult to believe by faith in your heart? The scriptures tells us, "Faith cometh by hearing…" In other words, faith appears when you **understand and agree** with the Word. The Apostle Paul talks about mature men and women who are able to understand the teaching of the Word based on their *senses* and *mental faculties*. There comes a time when believers must stand on the knowledge of the Word in total agreement and no longer rely on a childlike faith to produce what they want. Faith is the result of understanding and agreeing with the Word of God, what it says, and then, doing it.

Power Key: ***Agreement With The Holy Spirit And God's Word Results In Perfected Faith.***

In Hebrews 12:2, Jesus is the Author, Sustainer and Finisher of faith. There is a point when your faith graduates to completion. ***Your faith comes into agreement with the Word and is sustained and supported by what you know.*** The literal translation in the Greek for the word "finisher" means completeness, ***perfection***, growth, mental and moral character, conclusion, result, end, finally, utmost. Your faith can mature to a point where it is so complete that it reaches *perfection*. It is when the knowledge of the glory of God, the awareness of His Word, positions you for direct communion with the Holy Spirit. Verse four, in Chapter Six, of Hebrews talks about becoming a "sharer of the Holy Spirit". When you come into absolute agreement with the Word of God, your faith comes into completion and you enter a partnership with the Holy Spirit.

Partnership with the Holy Spirit means you are privy to what He sees. You do not need faith to see the "seen" when collaborating with the Holy Spirit.

Mature faith is believing for what you know is possible according to God's Word. When my wife was in the hospital on her deathbed, I knew the Word of God in my knowing, but I could not formulate it through my faith. My faith had given up, but the intellect of my spirit knew too much to refuse the knowledge of the Word.

~Spiritual Maturity~

A Journey Beyond Faith is the outcome of a disciplined life of faith. It is the synchronicity of the mind with the Word where the mind comes under the control of the Spirit: *"casting down vain imaginations and bringing into captivity every thought!"* This is when your mind, your spirit and your body align themselves with the Holy Spirit and you no longer function solely as a trichotomous being, but as a whole person. When a person is agreed within himself, he walks in a realm of total possibilities. It is like a melding of your three-part being; the more agreeable you are, the more in "oneness" you flow. In Mark 9:23, Jesus said, *"All things are possible to him that believeth."* The word *believeth* in the Greek, according to Strong's Concordance, means to **agree**. Anything is possible to you if you are in agreement.

You do not reach spiritual maturity until you are able to stay in agreement. You may be thinking that your situation is different; you were hurt and so you came out of agreement. After all, you are just a clump of clay on the potter's wheel. He is the potter you are the clay and so, you cry, "Mold me, shape me, make me Lord." I would like to know... WHEN DOES THE CLAY BECOME A POT? Once you become a pot for the Master's use, you attain to a new level of maturity. A clump of clay is no longer moldable when it is dry and shaped into a pot. It now becomes breakable. Are you still spinning around on the potter's wheel or are you ready to come into completion?

The favor of God is unlocked to the mature in faith. When your faith reaches maturity, you no longer need a cheering section. One interpretation of Hebrews 12:15 admonishes to live peaceably with everyone, so that no one will miss out on the ***special favor of God.*** The favor of God is contingent upon your willingness to walk in agreement with others.

~The Prayer Of Agreement~

James 5:15 reads, "…and the prayer of *faith* shall save the sick." The word faith in the Strong's Concordance, once again, is derived from the Greek word meaning *obey, yield, trust, make friend, confident and **agree**.* In other words, the prayer of ***agreement*** shall save the sick. This is deeper than a contingency on any one person's faith. ***It is a prayer of certainty, absolute agreement, and confidence in the knowledge of God.*** The prayer of agreement is simple. It is simply making known to God, our Father, that we understand and know that He is aware of what we know. And we know that for Him, nothing is impossible.

Faith** is having **peace** about what you **believe**.* Each one of the preceding underlined words come from the same Greek word meaning ***to agree. The prayer of faith is about a three fold absolute agreement. When you pray, simply say to God, "Father, I know, that You know, that I know, that anything is possible with You." That is confidence. That is a knowing beyond faith.

PRAYER OF AGREEMENT:

Dear Lord, I want to walk in absolute agreement with You. I want to know, that I know, that I know, beyond a shadow of a doubt that anything is possible with You. Take me on a journey beyond the faith I now have.
Amen

POWER KEY:

~The Marriage Of Faith And Agreement Produces The Unimaginable.
~Agreement With The Holy Spirit And God's Word Results In Perfected Faith.

MIA CULPA
"My Fault"

Power Key: *Divorce Is The Repugnant Act Of Covenant Breaking*.

ovenant agreement is as old as time and originated from God Himself. It is what Lucifer violated when he schemed with the angels trying to be like God. Moses called the violation of this covenant *divorcement*. The New Testament calls it *Covenant Breaking*. Americans know it as their way of escape from boredom. In addition, it stands to be one of the most overlooked sins within the Church. It is not a sin of external, visible consequence. Instead, it is an internal, abominable condition of the heart resulting in polluted, unacceptable worship to God. It becomes the nemesis of true worship.

Power Key: *The Nemesis Of Worship Is A Divided Heart.*

Turning a blind eye to the consequential ramifications, the leadership of the church stands by passively, as Christian couples desecrate the holiness of the marriage covenant. Unwittingly, the misinformed believers file into church, week after week, like mannequins with their pre-molded smiles having left half of their heart in the courtroom of some ungodly judge. Torn, shattered, divided, and blinded to their own condition, they fill the altars of worship in hopes that a Perfect, Righteous and Holy God of Covenant will accept their sacrifice of worship. *Malachi 2:13,17 (KJV), And this have ye done again, covering the altar of the Lord with tears, with weeping, and with crying out, insomuch that He regardeth not the offering any more, or receiveth it with good will at your hand. Ye have wearied the Lord with your words. Yet ye say, Wherein have we wearied Him? When ye say, Everyone that doeth evil is good in the sight of the Lord, and he delighteth in them; or Where is the God of judgment?*

A broken covenant…
A broken people…
A brokenhearted God…
The heart of God cries for true worshippers untainted by an apathetic tolerance of Covenant Breaking. The pollution found in the worship of the Church is not due to ungodly flesh; the flesh will always be at enmity with God, it is the issues of the heart, the

broken promises of the Church. It is the tolerance of divorce among marriages, among sexual unions, among pastors and sheep. The woman at the well, who had five husbands, was not hindered in her true worship because of her promiscuity, but because of her heart.

Men of God seldom broach the topic of divorce. Perhaps, because it is considered "too controversial... or not a good topic for the 21st century Church." Nevertheless, I would be greatly remiss writing this book if I cowardly shied away from the subject of divorce.

When two people come together, whether by marriage or by premarital sex, they have created a covenant agreement. It is apparent, when a marriage is terminated by divorce, the covenant has been broken. In the same manner, a covenant is broken when a relationship based on sex alone is terminated.

It is not enough to simply ask God to forgive the sin of divorce, then carry on as if nothing has changed. Everything changes when the foundation of two people's lives is uprooted. The foundation of marriage then, is not love. Love is the result of remaining in agreement.

Power Key: *It Was Agreement Before It Was Love.*

People can love each other and still end up in divorce if agreement is not the foundation of the marriage. Agreement then, is the support for every relationship. An environment is forever changed with the addition or subtraction of just one element. *Divorce is the disfigurement of the Bride of Christ.* The heathen have always desecrated the sanctity of the covenant. It is in their nature to break covenant, to give their word and not keep it. George Barna's poll data report on divorce among Born-again believers, as compared to Atheists, Agnostics and non-believers, ranks higher among Christians.

Born again believers..............27%
Not born-again.....................24%
Atheists, Agnostics...............21%

Divorce has become the demoralization of the Church. Ron Barrier, Spokesperson for American Atheists, remarked on these findings with some rather caustic comments against organized religion. He said: "These findings confirm what I have been saying these last five years. Since Atheist ethics are of a higher caliber than religious morals, it stands to reason that our families would be dedicated more to each other, than to some invisible monitor in the sky. With Atheism, women and men are equally responsible for a healthy marriage. There is no room in Atheist ethics for the type of 'submissive' nonsense preached by Baptists and other Christian and/or Jewish groups. Atheists reject, and rightly so, the primitive patriarchal attitudes so prevalent in many religions with respect to marriage."

You may think that an Atheist's comments have nothing to do with God's people. Yet, the sad reality is Atheists seem to have a clearer understanding about respecting one another than many believers.

It is disheartening to hear so many believers attacking the issues of abortion and homosexuality with no conviction about the rampant Covenant Breaking taking place within the Body of Christ.

The covenant of marriage and the Sabbath are the most ancient of divine ordinances. One might think, the oath of marriage is simply an ancient ritual. How can the Church disregard the principal of covenant, unless it should also ignore the Ten Commandments?

Marriage is an image of the divine romance between Christ and His Bride. It is not an invention made by men; it is the institution designed by God to produce godly offspring, seed, fruit, and increase. God will have nothing to do with anything that does not yield, increase or multiply. ***The absence of increase and multiplicity is proof something is lifeless.*** The first faculty bestowed to man was the power to perpetuate. God told Adam to be fruitful and multiply.

God hates divorce, because it is expropriation. It is the diminution of His plan for perpetuity. God never placed his approval on the act of divorce; it was a custom sanctioned by the Mosaic Law. God in His infinite mercy and compassion allowed divorce in the days of Moses, because man was hardhearted and evil. The husbands of that age were extremely brutal to their wives even unto death. These men were looking for a way to free themselves from the covenant of marriage. They were fearful of breaking covenant with God because of the consequences, yet, they disregarded the offensiveness of breaking covenant with their wives.

Malachi 2:16, For the Lord God, the God of Israel, says: I hate divorce and marital separation and him who covers his garment [his wife] with violence. Therefore keep a watch upon your spirit [that it may be controlled by My Spirit], that you deal not treacherously and faith-

lessly [with your marriage mate]. Larry Christenson comments in the Spirit Filled Bible, "When two people marry, God stands as a witness to the marriage, sealing it with the strongest possible word -- covenant. 'Covenant' speaks of faithfulness and enduring commitment. It stands as a divine sentinel over marriage, for blessing or for judgment."

When the Pharisees questioned Jesus in the Book of Matthew about divorce, He responded by pointing them back to the genesis of covenant. *Matthew 19:4-6, He replied, have you never read that He who made them from the beginning made them male and female, and said, for this reason a man shall leave his father and mother and shall be united firmly (joined inseparably) to his wife, and the two shall become one flesh? So they are no longer two, but one flesh. What therefore God hath joined together, let not man put asunder (separate).*

If God had intended divorce to be part of the design of man's life, He would have created more than one Eve for Adam to choose from. Instead, He made one Eve for one Adam and the two became one flesh. Adam said, "This is now bone of my bone and flesh of my flesh..." This is what Jesus was saying when He said, "Have you not read..."

Matthew Henry's commentary on the Whole Bible (by Hendrickson Publishers, Inc.) states: "The nature of the marriage contract; it is a union of persons; they twain shall be one flesh, so that they are no more twain, but one flesh. A man's children are pieces of himself, but his wife is himself." When God created man, He placed both male and female within him. Therefore, when a man divorces his wife, he severs part of himself. No wonder there are so many schizophrenic believers wandering from church to church.

In a movie my wife recently rented, a couple whose marriage is on the brink of divorce, decides upon their children's return from camp to inform them of their failed marriage. The final scene positions the couple waiting in a parking lot as the bus carrying their children, pulls up. The quiet time they share together in the car, prior to this scene, is filled with flashbacks of redolent memories.

When they greet the children, she is filled with the emotion of breaking the news while he masquerades the ugliness of divorce with laughter and jesting. He says, "let's go home." The children climb into their seats and she stands, at a distance, crying. He looks in her direction and she says, "Let's go to Chow Fun's." He replies, "We both agreed we can't really talk at Chow Fun." Without wasting a moment, she begins her monologue of recognizing her impending loss.

He speaks argumentatively and says, "Are you saying Chow Fun 'cause you can't face telling the kids? Because if that's why you're saying Chow Fun, then don't say Chow Fun."

She says, fighting back sobs, "No, that's not why Chow Fun. I'm saying Chow Fun, because we are an 'us'. There is a history here and histories don't happen over night. In Mesopotamia or Ancient Troy or somewhere back there, there are cities built on top of other cities. But I don't want to build another city. I like this city. I know where we keep the Bactine and what kind of mood you're in when you get up by which eyebrow is higher. And you always know that I'm a little quiet in the morning and compensate accordingly, that's a dance you learn over time. And it's hard, it's much harder than I thought it would be. But, there's more good than bad and you don't just give up! And it's not for the sake of the children, but gosh, they are great kids, aren't they? I mean, gosh, and we made them! I mean, think about that, there were no people, and then there were people, and they grew.

I won't be able to say to some stranger, 'Josh has your hands, or remember how Erin threw up at the Lincoln Memorial?'

Then I'll try to relax, and let's face it; anybody's gonna have traits that get on your nerves; I mean, why shouldn't it be *your* annoying traits? I'm no day at the beach, but I do have a good sense of direction, so at least I can find the beach. Which is not a criticism of yours, it's just a strength of mine.

You're a good friend and good friends are hard to find. Charlotte said that, in Charlotte's Web, and I love the way you read it to Erin. And you take on the voice of Wilbur the pig with such commitment, even when you're bone tired; that speaks volumes about character. And ultimately, isn't that what it comes down to? What a person's made of?"

She refers back to earlier in their marriage, when she laughed and goofed around wearing a Pittsburgh helmet.

She continues: "Because that girl in the Pitts helmet is still in here. (Pointing to her heart) I didn't even know she existed, until I met you. And I'm afraid if you leave, I may never see her again. Even though at times I said, you beat her out of me, isn't that the paradox?

Haven't we hit the essential paradox? Give and take, push and pull, Ying and Yang, the best of times, the worst of times. I guess what I'm trying to say, I'm saying Chow Fun's, 'cause I love you." They embrace and drive away with the entity called a family, that almost became a casualty.

In the closing scene, they are sitting on their sofa in their living room. They are playing a word game. He asks her to guess what seven-word phrase he is thinking of. She responds, saying, "…and they lived happily ever-after." He says, "That's six words." She says, "…and they lived mostly happily ever-after."

God intended for marriage to be forever. He never said it would be a "happily-ever-after" story. He did, however, install an "automatic-blessing-producer" into every marriage. He gave couples the Power of Agreement. "If any two shall agree, as touching anything, it shall be done of our Father who is in Heaven." God pronounced His favor upon the agreement of marriage.

Power Key: *Quitting Is Never An Option For A Winner.*

Perhaps, you have experienced the ravages of divorce and the wreckage of the shattered covenant clangs behind you.

Divorce is like a clanking chain announcing to

everyone the pain and rejection one has endured.

Maybe, it was not your fault.

The point is not deciding with whom the blame lies, rather, taking responsibility for another broken covenant. There is nothing gained by placing the blame solely on the other individual. A divorce takes two people consenting and agreeing to terminate a relationship that had its inception in love.

Perhaps, you have justified in your mind that divorce is acceptable. After all, "it is in my past. It's water under the bridge." You query in your own mind, without telling a soul, whether you did right or wrong.

I met a man the other day for the first time. He told me a little bit about himself and without any interrogation on my part, he spilled out his life story. He quickly divulged personal information about his divorce. We talked a little more about other topics and again he voiced his pain, "It wasn't my fault."

Here was a grown man in his early fifties, bantering like a four-year-old child, placing the blame on his wife alone. A Broken Covenant is the result of two people choosing to terminate their agreement.

The agreement between a man of God and a fellow minister is much like a marriage. One cannot just leave the other over a foolish argument. It is time for the Body of Christ to behave like Christ. The dismemberment of the Body is happening at an unprecedented rate, leaving the Church to appear like a person with multiple-personality-disorder. Work out your differences; find the agreeable factor. Destroy the disagreeable factor and part ways in peace, if you must. Stop the mutilation!

The agreement God made with His people was sprinkled with blood signifying the life of the covenant. A marriage agreement is a blood covenant. It is for life.

The children of Israel were notorious for their inconsistency in their relationship with the Lord. They were quick to complain about the conditions in the wilderness. They grumbled saying, "Would that we had died by the hand of the Lord in the land of Egypt…" God had been "waking up early" every morning preparing manna for them, and they were nagging and bellyaching.

Sound familiar?

How many marriages have ended in divorce over infantile squabbles?

How many pastor/protégé relationships have been terminated by the selfish, impish attitudes of insecure, immature, and envious young ministers, who think they know it all?

Personally speaking, I have had a few proteges who have "divorced" and abandoned me. They have forsaken a godly connection, all because they were unable to humble themselves and remain in the agreement.

*Exodus 24:1-3,7, God said to Moses, Come up to the Lord, you and Aaron, Nadab and Abihu [Aaron's sons], and seventy of Israel's elders, **worshipped at a distance.** Moses alone shall come near the Lord; the others shall not come near, and neither shall the people come up with him. Moses came and told the people all that the Lord had said and all the ordinances; and all the people answered with **one voice**, All that the Lord has spoken we will do. Then he took the **Book of the Covenant** and read in the hearing of the people; and they said, All that the*

Lord has said we will do, and we will be obedient.

The elders of Israel were not allowed to come up with Moses to worship. It was necessary for them to come into unity and agreement before they could have access to God's presence.

When an individual has Broken Covenant, whether in marriage or with divinely appointed people in their life, they have become tainted with the fragments of the Broken Covenant. It is these fragments that hinder the people of God from offering true worship. Without true worship, God cannot be properly accessed.

A Broken Covenant is like two people having been united by a beautiful vase with handles. When they decide to part ways, the only way out is to break the vase. They may ask God to forgive the sin of divorce. They may even part ways with feelings of mutual indifference. Either way:

At the root of every separation…

Every broken covenant…

Every aborted divine relationship...

Offense proudly boasts of, yet, another victory. It spreads its wings wide, creating a barrier between the soul and its Creator.

Power Key: *Worship Is The Lost Art Of A Soul's Cry For Its Creator.*

If you search deep within your soul, you will discover it is the root of offense that constrains your soul and keeps it from prospering. *III John 2, Behold, I pray that you may prosper in every way and [that your body]*

may keep well, even as [I know] your soul keeps well and prospers. The word **prosper** in the Greek means **road, highway, journey, progress, route, distance.** In other words prosper, progress, go the distance, stay on the right highway. The Broken Covenant puts you on the wrong highway. It detours you off the route you were assigned to, and sends you off alone.

I said earlier that divorce is the disfigurement of the Bride of Christ. The Broken Covenant among believers has caused a deviation from God's original plan.

When a believer offers up worship to God without taking responsibility for the refuse and debris of their shattered covenant, this becomes a personal affront to God. Lucifer's offense against God was his pride. This resulted in the breaking of the agreement within the perfect setting of Heaven. Every time someone lifts their voice in worship, God's attention is drawn to the breakage of their covenant. It would be like singing the song, "I love you Lord and I lift my voice…" Then adding in-between the verses, "Remember, how Lucifer broke covenant with you?"

In Malachi Chapter Two, God asks the question, *"Has it ever entered your mind that I was present when you made your covenant?"* (Paraphrase by author)

God is present at every wedding; He is there each time someone makes a commitment to a man or woman of God. He presides over the installation of a new associate pastor, elder, deacon, usher and Sunday School worker. He is present when adolescents yield to the pressure of premarital sex. God is watching us.

Greater than the sins of the flesh are the sins of Broken Covenant. *Luke 7:37, And behold, a woman of the town who was an especially wicked sinner, when she learned that He was reclining at table in the Pharisee's house, brought an alabaster flask of ointment (perfume), and standing behind Him at His feet weeping, she began to wet His feet with her [tears; and she wiped them with the hair of her head and kissed His feet affectionately] and anointed them with the ointment (perfume).* The woman of ill repute brought the mess of her Broken Covenant and offered it as a fragrant offering to the Lord. Her sins were forgiven, because she loved much.

Bring your shattered covenant to the Lord today. Take responsibility for the breakage. Do not waste time bantering back and forth trying to prove who is right and who is wrong.

Power Key: *Pride Is The Veil That Hides Truth And Falsely Misleads One To Self-justification.*

It is not easy admitting your divorce was just as much your fault as your spouse's. You may think, because you were the one who remained faithful to the vows and were chaste, that you would not be counted as a covenant-breaker. You must understand that the vows of marriage are not simply to remain faithful to one another but to the covenant of matrimony, as well. *Marriage is for life.*

Power Key: *Division Neutralizes The Power Of God.*

This chapter is not only for divorced couples...

It is for divorced pastors from their churches.

It is for divorced deacons from their pastors.

It is for divorced children from their parents.

It is for divorced, torn and shattered people sitting in churches all over the world.

I have often wondered, why so many people in the Church are sickly. Have you ever noticed that the largest ministries are healing ministries?

I Corinthians 11:27-30, So then whoever eats the bread or drinks the cup of the Lord in a way that is unworthy [of Him] will be guilty of [profaning and sinning against] the body and blood of the Lord. **That [careless and unworthy participation] is the reason many of you are weak and sickly,** *and quite enough of you have fallen into the sleep of death.* In this passage, people were partaking of the Lord's Supper which is the New Covenant in Christ, and all the while, harboring offense in their hearts. Offense and Covenant cannot coexist. Offense is sin committed against the Body of Christ, his Blood Covenant. Sickness comes upon those whose hearts are stained with the ominous deeds of offense.

The need for physical healings will greatly diminish when the problem with Broken Covenant is dealt with. Doctors have discovered that diseases, like arthritis and ulcers, are directly related to bitterness and unforgiveness.

James 5:12,14-16a, But above all [things], by brethren, do not swear, either by heaven or by earth or by any other oath; but let your yes be [a simple] yes, and

*your no be [a simple] no, so that you may not **sin** and fall into condemnation. Is anyone among you sick? He should call in the church elders (the spiritual guides). And they should pray over him, anointing him with oil in the Lord's name. And the prayer [that is] of faith will save him who is sick, and the Lord will restore him; and if he has committed sins, he will be forgiven. Confess to one another therefore your faults (your slips, your false steps, your **offenses**, your sins) and pray [also] for one another, that you may be healed and restored [to a spiritual tone of mind and heart].*

Many believers try to justify and diminish the offensiveness of Covenant Breaking. Allow me to give you an example of the filthiness of Covenant Breaking. Do you suppose God would have chosen Mary to carry His son if she had been a Covenant Breaker? Suppose, Mary had "known" a man in the biblical sense before her immaculate conception. Would you readily accept that her baby was the Son of the living God? Could it be you are struggling with the idea that the Holy Presence of God could never be housed in a Covenant Breaker? Still, God's people, the temples of His Spirit, casually enter in and out of covenant without any thought of what it does to the heart of God.

Power Key: ***Satan Cannot Violate The Boundaries Set By Our Agreement With God.***

As in the Book of James, the Word says, "Is any among you afflicted? Let him call upon the elders of the Church."

Are you afflicted?

Are you feeling guilty for Breaking Covenant?

Has the sting of offense become so deeply buried within you?

Have you masqueraded the pain behind justification?

Do you find yourself trying to make excuses for your actions?

"I'm not the one who quit!"

"I didn't ask for the divorce."

"The pastor didn't understand my vision and my goals. He didn't want me to go higher than him."

"The Broken Covenant, with my first husband, occurred when I was in the world and unsaved, so it doesn't count."

"I didn't get the raise I thought I deserved."

"My boyfriend said, if I didn't sleep with him, I didn't really love him."

"My mother and father never understood how much I needed them."

Regardless who is to blame, as I mentioned earlier in the chapter, there are broken pieces of your shattered vase that clank like chains around you.

I John 1:9, If we [freely] admit that we have sinned and confess our sins, He is faithful and just (true to His own nature and promises) and will forgive our sins [dismiss our lawlessness] and [continuously] cleanse us from all unrighteousness [everything not in conformity to His will and purpose and, thought, and action]. If we say (claim) we have not sinned, we contradict His word and make Him out to be false and a liar, and His Word is not

in us [the divine message of the Gospel is not in our hearts].

The first step to freedom from your Broken Covenants is to admit your involvement. I shared this message with a couple of people who have suffered divorce. They both wore the garments of self-justification. They were convinced their involvement in divorce was inconsequential. I shared with them how their signature, which completely nullified their agreement, made them liable. With the stroke of a pen, they had severed the bloodline of covenant. They had become people of bloodshed. In the Book of Romans a *covenant breaker* is listed among murderers. Unbeknownst to them, they were like dead people walking. Their willingness to right their wrong placed them in a readiness for the favor of God. *Romans 1:29-31 (KJV), Being filled with all unrighteousness, fornication, wickedness, covetousness maliciousness; full of envy, murder, debate, deceit, malignity; whisperers, backbiters, haters of God, despiteful, proud, boasters, inventors of evil things, disobedient to parents without understanding,* **covenantbreakers***, without natural affection, implacable, unmerciful;* Much of the sins listed in this passage are internal, unseen offenses. These are the sins which can separate the soul from its creator.

The Scripture, in I John, gives a step-by-step method for undoing the brokenness of shattered covenant.

You must first admit your guilt and take responsibility for the breakage. *Mia Culpa* are the Latin words for my fault. The Body of Christ must align itself with the message of agreement. Agreement is the absence of offense; it is the act of laying down one's dreams and embracing the dreams of another. It is a willingness to say, *Mia Culpa*; it is my fault! Jim Bakker, the former founder and president of the PTL Network, wrote a book entitled, "I Was Wrong". What a courageous act on his part, to state before the world that he was wrong. Was it entirely his fault? I disagree totally. My dear friend, Tammy Faye, his former wife, tells of the injustice that was done to the two of them. *Mia Culpa* takes the blame regardless who is to blame. Do not worry that your partner initiated your break up; instead, choose to take full responsibility. This requires humility on your part. It is not easy picking up someone else's mess. Jesus picked up your offenses and took them to the cross. Pick up the pieces of your Broken Covenants and take them to the altar of worship.

Confess your sin, your involvement. Ask for forgiveness and *break* yourself before the altar of worship.

God is looking for worshippers who will worship Him in Spirit and in truth. Now, you can worship in truth. You do not have to live a lie. You are free, you are delivered, and you are favored of the Lord!

Power Key: *Change Is Inevitable Through Worship.*

Power Key: *The Mark Of The Wise Is Humility Through Worship.*

Prayer of Agreement:

Heavenly Father of Covenant, I ask You to forgive me for all the broken covenants aware and unaware in my life. Take the broken pieces as I lift them up to You, as an offering of worship. Dear God, I confess it is "my fault." I take full responsibility for each relationship in my life. In the Name of the Father, the Son, and the Holy Spirit; Three in One.

Amen

Power Keys:

~Divorce Is The Repugnant Act Of Covenant Breaking.
~The Nemesis Of Worship Is A Divided Heart.
~It Was Agreement Before It Was Love.
~Quitting Is Never An Option For A Winner.
~Worship Is The Lost Art Of A Soul's Cry For Its Creator.
~Pride Is The Veil That Hides Truth And Falsely Misleads One To Self-justification.
~Division Neutralizes The Power Of God.
~Satan Cannot Violate The Boundaries Set By Our Agreement With God.
~Change Is Inevitable Through Worship.
~The Mark Of The Wise Is Humility Through Worship.

~21~

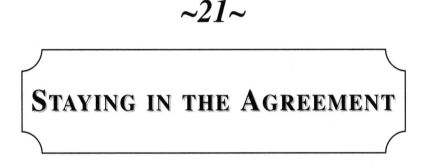

STAYING IN THE AGREEMENT

Power Key: *There Is No Success Outside Of Agreement.*

greement is never-ending. You must stay in the race to win the prize. One of the first covenant Agreements God made with man was with Abraham. Thousands of years after the initial Agreement, the *Covenant of Blessings* still lives on for our children, our children's children, and us. The *Covenant of Blessings* need not ever stop. *Galatians 6:9, And let us not be weary in well doing: for in due season we shall reap, if we faint not.* This present generation's willingness to remain in agreement is its only preservation. The Church understands and receives the blessings of prosperity today, because of the agreement between one man and God.

Agreement is never-ending; it is forever. Eternal. Just as the Father, Son and Holy Spirit function in a continuous circle of love, unity, and humility, submitted One to Another; we must do the same with one another. Your consistent desire to walk in agreement becomes the evidential proof of the "Eternal One" living within you.

Choose to *Stay in the Agreement*.

As difficult as coming into agreement and finding the agreeable factor may be, staying in the agreement is usually the toughest part. A famous actor once said, "Growing old isn't for sissies," neither is staying in the agreement.

Power Key: *Quitting Is Never An Option For A Winner!*

Staying in the Agreement requires perseverance, stamina and a continuous commitment to growth. It requires faith and a complete reliance on God. Above all, it requires humility, honoring the agreement and hanging tough when the going gets tough.

I knew a man who got a whopping credit card bill one month. He was irate, assured that the company had made a mistake or was trying to rip him off. Photocopies of every purchase, along with receipts, which included my friend's signature, accompanied his monthly statement.

"How can I dispute it?" my friend laughed. "There's my signature on every single one of those receipts!"

With every purchase, he had signed his name, in essence, agreeing to later pay for the purchase. He wanted to break the Agreement when the going got tough.

Agreement is not a one-time thing. It is continual. Agreement is more than a verbal promise; it is a contractual pact that has a life of its own. Like Abraham, you must learn to come into Agreement with the vision God has for your life. Abraham gained the understanding, over the years, that God was faithful to His promises and to His Agreement. *Deuteronomy 7:9 (KJV), The Lord thy God, He is God, the faithful God, which keepeth covenant and mercy with them that love Him.*

Numbers 23:19, God is not a man that He should lie, nor a son of man . . .

Every Agreement has a promise, but to see the fulfillment of the promise, you have to fulfill the obligation. To own a car, you have to make 48 or 60 months of payments. Agreement's foundation must be faith, not feelings. Whatever excites you now, eventually, can make you miserable. A new car is wonderful, until you have to start making the payments. The honeymoon of marriage is wonderful, but then, you have to learn how to live with your new spouse. You must fulfill your end of the agreement with the bank that financed your car and walk out the four or five years of agreement. You must learn to walk humbly and lovingly with your spouse in marriage.

Offense and disagreement abort miracles and thwart God's plans. When you come out of agreement, you fatefully leave the essence of the Trinity.

Power Key: *Coming Out Of Agreement Is Coming Out Of The Spirit.*

The fruit of agreement does not become evident overnight. As badly as you want your breakthrough, you have to wait for it to reach full maturation. If you break an agreement before it flourishes into fruitfulness, you will lose the blessings that would, ultimately, have been yours. As was discussed in Chapter Two, you can become offended at your great peril. The smallest of offenses can grow into calamities.

Proverbs says, "A brother offended is harder to win than a fortified city." If you do not, tenaciously, tend to the little weeds of disagreement in your heart, they may grow into mighty fortresses of offense that may defy your efforts of being torn down. When you allow a negative thought to linger in your mind, you then require a deliverer as opposed to just following a simple instruction. II Corinthians 10:5 says, *"Casting down every vain imagination..."* When offense goes from a fleeting thought of anger in your mind and festers in your heart, you have opened yourself to the dangers of demonic manipulation.

Consider the sad case of Ananias and Sapphira in Acts 5. As was discussed earlier in the book, the early church abounded in agreement. Believers were so full of the fruit of the Spirit that they willingly gave up land and possessions, so that all could share and have sufficiency.

Ananias and Sapphira broke this spirit of agreement by holding back part of the money they received for the property they sold. *Acts 5:3-4 (KJV), But Peter said,*

Ananias, why hath Satan filled thine heart to lie to the Holy Ghost, and to keep back part of the price of the land. While it remained, was it not thine own? And after it was sold, was it not in thine own power? Why hast thou conceived this thing in thine heart? Thou has not lied unto men, but unto God.

When you come out of agreement with man, you are coming out of agreement with God. The price can be prohibitively high. In the case of Ananias and Sapphira, it cost them their lives. Am I saying that you will drop dead if you break agreement with someone? No. Nevertheless, many of the dreams and miracles you may be hoping for may fall by the wayside.

My dear and long time friend, Dr. Mike Murdock, tells a story of sowing a sizeable seed to Dr. Oral Roberts. Roberts held his hand tightly and said, "I'm not coming out of the agreement." Murdock responded, "OK," Dr. Roberts clung to Murdock's hand and kept repeating, "I'm not coming out of the agreement." Finally, Dr. Murdock realized Roberts was asking him to come into agreement – into a covenant – with him.

One of the great "agreements" in the Bible, was between Ruth and Naomi. Ruth's whole destiny was wrapped up in her agreement with Naomi, her mother-in-law. When the book of Ruth opens, Naomi and Ruth are in a bleak situation. Ruth's husband and Naomi's sons are all dead. The desolate and embittered Naomi urges Ruth to go back to her family. Indeed, it seems like a good idea. Remember, this is the same woman, whom the Bible says, was filled with offense; she changed her name to "bitterness." Imagine your in-laws being known for their bitter attitudes and you insisting to embrace them as your own. There is no greater story depicting the essence of agreement than when Ruth embraces Naomi's somewhat dismal dream and turns out a champion.

The story goes on to say, Ruth agreed with Naomi and forsook all that was familiar and embraced a strange land, people, and religion. In one of the Bible's great anthems of agreement – read at thousands of weddings each year as couples agree to be loyal to one another – Ruth declares her allegiance to Naomi in *Ruth 1:16 (KJV),*

> *ENTREAT ME NOT TO LEAVE THEE.*
> *WHITHER THOU GOEST I WILL GO.*
> *WHITHER THOU LODGEST, I WILL LODGE.*
> *THY PEOPLE SHALL BE MY PEOPLE,*
> *THY GOD MY GOD.*

Ruth found the Agreeable Factor; she embraced Naomi's dream, nation and her God. Talk about costly!

Although, she found the Agreeable Factor, the blessings did not come to Ruth instantly. This is something you must be aware of as you seek to find the agreeable factor. Agreement often requires a season of waiting. *Patience is the catalyst that carries the seed of agreement from hope to manifestation.* Ruth endured a season of gossip, uncertainty and lack, but she clung to her agreement with Naomi.

Power Key: *The Fruit Of Agreement Is Favor.*

Ruth's decision to stay in agreement with her mother-in-law produced the delicious fruit of favor. While tending fields, Ruth was being observed by the well-to-do kinsman, Boaz. Of all the young women who plied his fields, Ruth stood out to him, because of her agreement with Naomi. *Ruth 2:10-11, Then she fell on her face, bowing to the ground and said to him, 'Why have I found favor in your sight that you should take notice of me, since I am a foreigner?' And Boaz answered and said to her, All that you have done for your mother-in-law after the death of your husband has been fully reported to me, and how you left your father and your mother and the land of your birth, and came to a people that you did not previously know.*

Ruth laid down her dreams for Naomi. Her stubborn adherence to Naomi was the key that unlocked everything for Ruth: a wonderful husband, beautiful children, financial security – and the choicest prize of all, God Himself. When Ruth intones the beautiful monologue of agreement; she embraces Naomi's homeland, her people and ultimately her God. Ruth pronounced a curse upon herself if she were to ever come out of agreement with her mother-in-law Naomi. **Agreement is a serious commitment.**

Remember our key verse: *Matthew 18:19, Again I say to you that if two of you **agree** on earth concerning anything that they ask, it will be done for them by My Father in heaven.*

You agree on earth, but the Father in heaven does all the work. It is based on what you can agree upon on earth. Your obligation is to simply agree on earth and

Jesus stands at the right hand of the Father interceding on your behalf.

You must agree in the name of Jesus; there is no other name. He is the way; He is the common denominator – the ultimate Agreeable Factor. No matter what pettiness and sin separates believers, there can always be unity in His precious name. *Philippians 2:10,11, Every knee shall bow and every tongue confess that Jesus Christ is Lord.*

I am persuaded, if believers would come into agreement – **and stay** – the greatest move of the Holy Spirit in the history of the church would be released. The power unleashed will create its own momentum, leaving no room for offense.

The Power of Agreement is the greatest anointing on earth. It is the movement among believers that will usher in the second coming of Christ – the great day when we all will bow our knees and confess that Jesus Christ is Lord. ***The anointing of agreement releases the nature of the Spirit; it is the absence of offense.***

Ephesians 4:4-6, [There is] one body and one Spirit-just as there is also one hope [that belongs] to the calling you received- there is one Lord, one faith, one baptism, One God and Father of [us] all, Who is above all [Sovereign overall], pervading all and [living] in [us] all. Agreement eliminates the guesswork of what to believe and what not to. When you agree there is one Lord, one faith, one baptism, and one Father; it leaves no room for confusion which could lead to offense. Remember, offense is the original sin. God is a God of love. He will forgive any sin confessed. Offense is a mystery for most Christians and herein lies the problem. *It is the secret power of lawlessness that separates us from the perfectness of God.*

Go for it! Agree with one another. Prepare yourself for that great day when the redeemed dwell entirely in the essence of the Father, Son and Holy Spirit. In absolute agreement. Are we agreed?

PRAYER OF AGREEMENT:

Lord, Help me to delight myself in Your Word, so I will never be offended. I know that offense is the enemy of agreement and I pray by Your Spirit that I will have a pure heart. I choose to walk in agreement and will be careful not to offend others, in Your Name I pray.

Amen

POWER KEYS :

~There Is No Success Outside Of Agreement.
~Quitting Is Never An Option For A Winner.
~Coming Out Of Agreement Is Coming Out Of The Spirit.
~The Fruit Of Agreement Is Favor.

~22~

A FAIRYTALE OF FAVOR
"A TRUE STORY"

I love reading books with out-of-this-world endings. So, I decided to write a fairy tale with a "they-lived-happily-ever-after" ending. How good would a book about the favor of God be if it did not have an out-of-this-world true account of His goodness? The Favor of God is real! It is not complicated to unlock. The Favor of God is made available to every believer who chooses to walk in agreement. I am not shocked that the Holy Spirit led me to end this profound book on the Agreement with the innocence and simplistic beliefs of a child.

Agreeability is made easier when you approach it from a childlike mentality. Children quickly forgive and quickly forget the wrongs done by their peers. A child is naïve and trusting believing almost anything. I have a six-year old and a nine-year old who just visited the North Pole in Colorado. My nine-year old became very flustered when she sat on the lap of the "real" Santa Claus. Santa asked her how old she was and she answered, "Six". My little six-year-old-man could hardly look at him. He was convinced he was the true Santa. This was in the middle of July. Their surroundings and the climate had nothing to do with their belief of Santa Claus. They know Santa is confined to circumstantial scheduling. He was in between seasons, but that made him no less real in their eyes.

The favor of God is not a garment you put on every morning, rather, it is an attitude you exude which causes God and man to become one. That is what I call **Absolute Agreement!** *Matthew 18:2-4, And He called a little child to Himself and put him in the midst of them, and said, Truly I say to you, unless you repent (change, turn about) and become like little children trusting, lowly, loving, forgiving], you can never enter the kingdom of Heaven [at all]. Whoever will humble himself therefore and become like this little child [trusting, lowly, loving, forgiving] is greatest in the kingdom of heaven.* And now, my fairytale…

Once upon a time in a not so far away land, there lived a boy named … well, names are not important. But what happened to this lad you'll scarcely believe! He grew up with three brothers and three sisters.

His brothers were mostly unkind…

And ridiculed him because of his mind. For in his mind this boy knew
there was something different. He knew what to do!

One day he decided that a piano he'd play...
And what do you know? It is just as I say...
He played and he played, then he played for the King.
The King was delighted and gave him a ring. Then He
clothed him with garments of praise and with song.
He put a robe on his back and He said, "Run along."
A song of praise, a song of love,
he played and he sang to the King up above.

Then one day the boy met a girl.
You can imagine what he thought as she smiled-and sent
him on a whirl.
The boy and the girl fell in love right away. They decided to
marry and oh, what a day!

She wore a beautiful white gown and he wore a white
suit. Down the aisle of the chapel she walked...
and oh, what a sight!
It was so right.

This was no ordinary couple; for they believed with all
their hearts, they were meant for each other. They went

before the altar of the Lord and sang their songs of love.
That day they vowed that from each other they would never
part.
It was an agreement of love that they signed with their
blood...
with a song and a prayer God's throne they did flood.

From two diverse backgrounds originated this union. He
came from a large family with lots of loud talking, with no
scheduled suppers around the table. His was a simple life,
with never a dull moment. She, on the other hand was like
something straight out of "Leave It To Beaver". Though
they had very little, as far as worldly possessions, they did
have their talents. And both agreed those talents belonged
to the Lord.

On every day matters, they seldom agreed. They were
like black and white. When he was up, she was down. If
she was in, he was out. The two were like night and day.
But their love was strong; and you know what they say,
"love conquers all." Their ship of love had sailed. Surely,
they could weather any storm.
Whenever their skies turned gray,
and they felt at times, they had lost their way. Their songs
of worship could always lead the way.
Worship was the agreeable factor. Together they made

music that brought people to their knees. She had a voice like an angel and his roared like a lion. This angel and lion made music together and every one applauded and gave their approval.

There life together was blossoming like a beautiful flower in the bounty of spring. Certain that things could only get better, they braced themselves for the adventure.

Then early one morning the girl became quite ill. She called out for the man. He came and found her in bed, lying on her back, racked with intense pain. With a look of consternation and fear of impending danger, he whisked her away. He had seen her through the difficulty of two miscarriages and two life-threatening surgeries. Now, not only did the signs point to great danger for her life, but also for the baby she carried inside.

A prophetess came to town and spoke of the blessing of this baby.
She confirmed with no sonograms that this was a boy-baby.
She told of the joy he would bring...
and everything he would mean.

They were already blessed with a beautiful little girl, who at times had been their only real joy amidst the storms they

encountered. Whatever happened to their ship of love that set
sail, and could endure any storm? Where did they go
wrong?

The prophetess said the baby inside would be the completion
of many things that had been taken from the two, while
fighting on the front lines for their King.

In times past God had spoken through the little girl. One
night this man sat alone in the dark, in his study. Feeling
alone and deserted, in the throws of defeat because those
closest to him had turned against him. The three-year-old
sat on her daddy's lap, wiping his tears away and said,
"Those people are nothing but a bunch of hyenas."
Her comment caused laughter to mingle with tears,
renewing his hope, it rid him of fears.

Once on another occasion she had exhorted him, again
with her childish philosophy and said, "You know daddy,
sometimes our cookies just don't turn out the way we want
them to." This man's cookies were burning.
He looked for confirmation that all would be well,
but this time the little angel had nothing to tell.

Would God speak His Word and put an end to this
whole ordeal before it began?
A trip to the ER turned dismal in minutes, when doctors
decided at four in the morning they would have to perform

emergency surgery, leaving no hope for the six and a half month old baby still in the womb. The nightmare had begun...

The man pondered the fear-filled words the doctors spoke. The fate of his wife and their promised child was in the hands of mere men. The choice was not much of a choice at all. Save her and lose the promise. Protect the promise and lose her. If there was anything this man had learned during those first trying years; was, never to move when where to go he did not know. And so, he waited. Not on doctors, who see only what is seen. He waited on the One who sees what is, what was, and what is to come.

Two weeks in ICU and nine specialists later, still unable to pinpoint or diagnose the problem....

A shadow appeared.

A shadow of death?

A shadow of fear?

Or was it a shadow of Someone come near?

A thread of hope, or ray of sunshine?

It was more than that, It was a Promise Divine.

Though thin and wispy, or so it appeared, whatever this shadow, they welcomed it near. For in the heat of adversity, though shadows be dark, they bring their relief, like a walk in the park.

And on the eve of the woman's birthday, the ray of light, which found its way through the darkness, gave hope that tomorrow would be so much brighter.
Friends of the couple readied themselves for celebration; not only for her birthday...but also for the hope God had given for two precious lives that hung in the balance.

Balloons and cake were ordered. Their little girl was summoned and scheduled to make a visit for the first time since her mommy had taken ill. The doctors brought hope of a private room.
The hopeful couple would fill it with joy and laughter, with flowers and friends filled to the rafters.
This would be one of the happiest birthdays ever; she was out of the woods now.

Sleeping in chairs and on cold, damp floors, the man had promised himself never to leave her side. And often he recalled their solemn promise, that from each other they would never part.
When walls and doors between them came, he would find a window and watch over her just the same.

Excited about the hopeful news, the man lay down and rested for the first time since that day his wife had cried out in pain. No sooner had he dozed off, when one of his friends came running with news that something was wrong.

Because this was an intensive care unit
there was no visiting before or after the appointed times;
regardless of how desperate the situation.
He quickly arose from his crouched position and ran to the
window across a corridor that separated the wing where she
lay and the waiting room where he stayed.

It had been just an hour since he peered through the
window... He had waited till his wife sound asleep she had
fallen. And now, that peaceful, serene scene of his wife and
the child sleeping... had become distorted and chaotic.
His wife began flailing all over the bed; nurses scurried and
hurried working to place restraints on her wrists and feet.
He watched as his partner was tied down like some crazed
animal, and he could do nothing. He was powerless.
His mind raced as he thought of the plans that had been
made. Their little girl would be showing up in just a matter
of hours.
He watched helplessly from the window. When he could
take no more, he boldly marched beyond the doors that had
distanced him from his love, and he took charge. The attending nurse and head nurse were at the front desk, and followed the man with their eyes as he marched into her room.
There was something so strong pulling on him. It was

deeper than love; it was stronger than desire. It was Agreement.

The man walked into a presence so strong.
It had accompanied many in this very room as they had moved on.
From this life to the next life with no hope of return. Dark and clammy... It had a bone~chilling feeling that moved about without a sound.

The man climbed high into bed with his wife, he held her in his arms and he loved her with all his might.
Unable to talk with her, he sang her a song. And then tried again and again to talk with his friend. But he could not a word from her withdraw.
This sickness so wicked, had taken her thoughts and separated her far from him, so she could not talk.

He sang of the one who had witnessed their vows...
he sang over, and over until she made a sound. She opened her mouth and she sang out a song. and the two harmonized just as they did when all was all right.
And then without notice the presence he had felt, distorted their sounds. Bells began ringing and monitors went off.
Then doctors came running because her heart had now stopped....

they ushered the man out and gave him no hope. his wife
now lay dead...
the double doors behind him slammed, like iron gates, too
heavy to move, they wedged between he and his love.

"Oh faith, why have you failed me now?" he cried. "i
stood on the Word of the One in the Shadow. he said, it
would be like a walk in the park."
The birthday plans, the friendship plans. the little girl
coming to visit... was now just a memory, a memory of love.
then deep down inside this man, as if powered from above,
something awakened and he knew that this was more than
just love.
it was once again deeper and came from above.
a power, a knowing, the promise of life,
the agreement they made at the start of their life...
had taken them past the perils of life.

and the baby of promise came just as was told,
he was healthy and handsome and cuddly to
hold.
the lady, the baby, the little girl too,
came home to their father and
started anew.
The Power of Agreement worked for the two,
who had vowed to each other.... "Truly, I do..."

The fairytale you have just read is a true story. It is more than a love story…

It is a beautiful account of the power, the force, the strength of *agreement*…

It is a demonstration of a love so deeply rooted in *agreement*…

It is a demonstration of the favor of *agreement*…

It is a demonstration of the unity in the Godhead and their desire for a Bride that operates in *Agreement*…

It is why I wrote this book, because without *Agreement* there can be no true worship. Worship is the lost art of a soul crying out for its Creator.

TESTIMONIES

After hearing all the teaching on "The Power of Agreement" and applying it to my everyday life, I have seen more order and peace in my home. My daughter and I, who have had many problems and disagreements in the past, are now walking in harmony. Now, whenever I feel offended, instead of hanging on to it, I quickly deal with it and release it.

My new attitude of agreement has brought me much favor in my career.
Yolanda Cogswell
Mansfield, TX

Since I have come into agreement with Pastor Thomas and his teaching. I have seen great changes in every area of my life. Because I am seeking and finding the agreeable factor with my family and others, my walk with God is advancing. I have joined the Friday night prayer group. After prayer and staying in agreement for God to make a way for us to buy a house, we now own our first home since we came to Texas. I know this was only possible, because of the power of agreement.
Francis and Jessica Hudson
Arlington, TX

Seven years ago I came into agreement with the prophetic and knew God had a great plan for my life, in Texas. I began studying, staying in agreement with my pastor in California, and serving great men and women of God in my church. In the fullness of time, God moved me to Texas, where I became the Executive Assistant to Pastor Thomas Michael, and to live in the Las Colinas resort, He had shown me before. I stayed in agreement with what I knew was God's Voice. When I first learned of the Power of Agreement in June of '99, I sowed a seed, and just a few months later, received the *gifts* of a beautiful car, computer and cordless phone that I had asked God for. The Power of Agreement works, as I have experienced answered prayers and blessings of favor like never imagined.
Melanie Hart
Irving, TX

In May, my brother was being sued by a neighbor, who was upset because my brother's new house on the beach was obstructing his view. He was paying attorneys fees of $3000.00 per month for over a year, to

protect himself. He was ready to give in to the suit, when my husband and I came into agreement for God to do something about the pressure my brother was under. Three days after we prayed, a developer offered to pay all the legal expenses from that moment on.
Luis and Pam Pereira
Arlington, TX

Pastor Thomas,

I cannot begin to tell you how much the teaching on divorce, separation, division, the breaking of covenant and coming out of agreement has touched my heart and inner soul. This is a place where I tend to hold everything inside that I don't want to talk about or that if I leave alone will eventually be okay. I had to face the fact that I have been placing the blame on my husband for his actions, that I believe was the cause for our divorce. You said, "two wrongs don't make a right." So , it is up to me to say, God it's my fault. I can only begin to think of the worship I have been offering up to God has been tainted. Now I have picked up the broken pieces and cleaned up our mess and now I can give God the true worship He desires. This day has brought healing and a new beginning of the things that God desires for me. I feel ten pounds lighter. I want the whole world to hear this message.
Virginia Martinez
Arlington, TX

Twenty-one years ago an IRS debt was incurred by my spouse, leaving me responsible to pay after our divorce. I began making payments of $25.00 per month. By the year 2000 the debt had grown to over $30,000.00. I thought this would be a debt I could never possibly pay off.

After Pastor Thomas began teaching about the Power of Agreement, I sowed a seed of $500.00 for the unexpected. Shortly after this I wrote the IRS informing them I had not received my usual payment schedule. Consequently, I sent my regular payment of $25.00 with my letter.

Miraculously, I received a letter back from the IRS stating the debt had been cleared and I owed nothing.

Praise the Lord for the Power of Agreement!
Ann Hill
Arlington, TX

ENDORSEMENTS

"Pastor Thomas Michael is a diligent student of the Bible; an able 'proclaimer of the Word'. He is a most talented musician, both instrumental and vocal. Both personally and professionally, I recommend him as a preacher and as a 'sweet singer of Israel'. He is a servant of our Lord Jesus Christ with few equals."
Rev. E. H. Jim Ammerman, Th.D., D.D. President C.F.G.C.

"Pastor Thomas Michael is a valued, treasured, choice friend and my personal Pastor, whom never fails to show the nature of Jesus Christ. I have seen the glory of God fill the house when Thomas Michael begins to minister. God makes him a golden link as the people come out of where they are into a glorious place with God. He has an elegance, a dignity, a purity, integrity and a stability about him that will never make you ashamed."
Dr. Mike Murdock, Author, Evangelist, Teacher, Songwriter

"This book, on the Power of Agreement, is a book of treasure! Every potential leader or servant of God, national or international, must read this. What a tremendous revelation God has given to my friend, Pastor Thomas Michael. You and your vision will never be the same."
H.M. King Ayi
Traditional Symbolic King from Togo, West Africa

"Pastor Thomas Michael and his lovely wife, Judy, have been both guests and hosts at Daystar TV Network. They are my two favorite singers in the whole world."
Joni Lamb, Co-founder of Daystar TV Ch. 29, Recording Artist

"Pastor Thomas and Judy are real people. I have never met anyone like them in all my years of ministry and travel. Their musical talents and abilities far exceed anything I have ever seen on Broadway or Hollywood. Pastor Thomas has the exceptional ability to hold captive my attention, making me breathless in anticipation of what God is about to do next."
Rev. Tammy Faye Messner, First Lady of Christian TV, Singer, Evangelist, TV Personality

"I have never seen anyone operate under a more tremendous anointing as God's Instrument of Worship than Thomas Michael. His unique ability to articulate God's Word through song, literally, ushers people into the presence of God like nothing else I have ever seen or experienced in my 12 years as a full-time evangelist. My wife and I are both blessed beyond measure every time we hear him minister in word and song."
Rev. Lowell Mims, Evangelist

Bibliography

Conner, Kevin J. Interpreting the Symbols and Types. Bible Temple Publishing, Portland, Oregon, 1992.

Hayford, Litt.D., Jack W. Spirit Filled Life Bible-New King James Version, Thomas Nelson Publishers, Nashville, Tennessee, 1991.

Henry, Matthew. Commentary on the Whole Bible: New Modern Edition, Electronic Database. Hendrickson Publishers, Inc., 1991.

Murdock, Mike. The Law of Recognition, Wisdom International, Dallas, Texas, 1999.

Strong, S.T.D., LL.D, James. The Exhaustive Concordance of the Bible, Riverside Book and Bible House, Iowa Falls, Iowa.

SALVATION DECISION

The Bible says, "For all have sinned, and come short of the glory of God…" (Rom. 3:23). No one person has ever, or will ever be able to enter the kingdom of Heaven based on their own efforts. Eternal security comes only from an agreement with the Word of God. "That if thou shalt confess with thy mouth the Lord Jesus, and shalt believe in thine heart that God hath raised him from the dead, thou shalt be saved." (Rom. 10:9)

To receive Jesus Christ as your Lord and Savior, may I invite you to pray the prayer of agreement for salvation?

"Dear Jesus, I believe in my heart that You died for me, and that You rose again on the third day. I confess with my mouth that You are the Lord. Come into my life and forgive me of my sins. Create in me a clean heart and renew in me an agreeable spirit that I might worship the Father in Spirit and in truth. Thank You for Your presence, in which there is peace, joy, and love. In the Name of the Father, the Son, and the Holy Ghost.
Amen."

Please write and let me know of your salvation decision.

PASTOR THOMAS MICHAEL
c/o POWER CHURCH
702 GREENVIEW DR.
GRAND PRAIRIE, TX 75050

CIRCLE OF AGREEMENT PARTNER

Dear Partner,
The act of agreement with this ministry will change your life forever! I know God has brought you to this threshold of favor and prosperity in order to bless you and your loved ones.
Will you become an "Agreement Partner" with me? Your seed can be the agreeable factor between you and I. When you sow the seed of agreement with a man of God you will unlock the favor of God, activate the unexpected, and release uncommon prosperity into your life.

"Believe (agree with) the Lord your God and you shall be established; believe (agree with) and remain steadfast (stay in agreement) with His prophets and you shall prosper" II Chronicles 20:20 (AMP paraphrased)

POWER KEY: *Agreement With a Man of God is More Valuable Than Your Harvest, Because He is the Connection to Your Harvest.*

Platinum Agreement Partner (Enclosed is my first monthly seed of $300.00 to unlock the favor of God).

Gold Agreement Partner (Enclosed is my first monthly seed of $100.00 to release uncommon prosperity).

Silver Agreement Partner(Enclosed is my first monthly seed of $30.00 to activate the unexpected).

Agreement Seed (Enclosed is my seed of $_____)

NAME	
ADDRESS	
CITY/STATE/ZIP	
MC/VISA/AMER. EXPRESS #	EXP.
SIGNATURE	

MAIL CHECK, MONEY ORDER, OR CHARGE INFO TO:
POWER CHURCH P.O. BOX 200367-ARLINGTON, TX 76006
PHONE: 972-336-0222 FAX: 972-641-7374 EMAIL: APOWERCHURCH@AOL.COM

MUSIC CD'S BY THOMAS MICHAEL

Self titled CD with hits such as, Greater Love, It's Your Glory, Could You Be The One, and Messiah.

A collection of moments in His presense; dedicated Pastors Joe and Linda Knight, and the passengers of Alaskian Airlines flight 261.

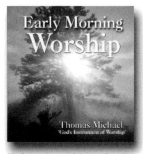

The first in a live recorded series of worship to the Holy Spirit.

This Instrumental CD will take you through the Winter, Spring, Summer and Fall of your life.

The second in a live recorded series of worship to the Holy Spirit.

A collection of mayestic songs and truimphant melodies.

TEACHING SERIES BY THOMAS MICHAEL

The Power Of Agreement

 With his inimitable, in-your-face style, Pastor Thomas Michael will reveal the most powerful anointing on the earth today. Agreement is the union by which the Father, Son, and Holy Ghost operate: and it is the sys tem by which all things are created.

A Woman's Freedom from the Curse

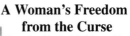 Through this insightful teaching, Pastor Thomas helps bring healing to women who are at war with their emotions. Learn why women are afflicted with physical and emotional problems such as PMS, breast cancer, menopause, and how to overcome these problems.

The Partner

 The Partner is an in-depth look at the person of the Holy Spirit. This teaching series lays the foundation for a proper relationship with the Holy Spirit. It will unlock the functions, abilities, and the power of the Holy Spirit, seldom accessed by the believer.

The Law of Order

 Special moments with the Holy Spirit are lost everyday because of the disorder in people's environments. Pastor Thomas will challenge the order in your life and home, and will expose the hidden areas of chaos and disorder. *The Realm of the Spirit is Order.*" (Power Key 2000)

God Confidence

 Pastor Thomas teaches the church to, "Cast not away therefore your confidence, which has great recompense of reward." God Confidence means going beyond religion into an intimate relationship through obedience rather than performance..

Our Precious Faith

Our Precious Faith is a revelatory message given to Pastor Thomas while standing at the Wailing Wall in the Holy Land. This series will make clear the true purpose of your faith and the power in the faith of those who have not seen yet, still believe.

The Anointed One

When your relationships are failing, when the weight of your finances overwhelms you, and your dreams have been shattered, it is the Anointed One and His Anointing that will destroy the yoke of bondage over your life.

The Secret Power of Lawlessness

 In the perfected state of Heaven...amidst the streets paved with gold...the SECRET power of lawlessness found its way into the heart of Lucifer. This same power is secretly working in the hearts of believers who have allowed OFFENSE to silence their worship.

PRODUCT ORDER FORM

Quantity	Description	CD	Tape	Total
	Thomas Michael	$15.00	$11.00	
	Early Morning Worship I	$15.00	$11.00	
	Early Morning Worship II	$15.00	$11.00	
	Early Morning Worship III		$11.00	
	Seasons of Love	$15.00	$11.00	
	You're My Praise	$15.00	$11.00	
	Piano Praise		$11.00	
	Special Moments In His Presence	$15.00		
	Thomas Michael Tracks		$12.00	
	TEACHING SERIES	**BOOK**	**TAPES**	
	The Secret Power of Lawlessness		$40.00	
	The Power of Agreement		$55.00	
	The Law of Order		$30.00	
	The Partner-A Discovery of the Holy Spirit		$60.00	
	The Anointed One		$60.00	
	God Confidence		$60.00	
	A Woman's Freedom From The Curse		$20.00	
	Healing of the Races		$15.00	
	Our Precious Faith		$40.00	
	The Just Shall Live By Faith		$25.00	
	Battle of the Bruised		$25.00	
	The Stirring of the Waters		$10.00	
	Keys to the Kingdom		$20.00	
	Charting a Prophetic Path		$25.00	
	Prosperity Through God's Word		$15.00	
	Acquiring a High View of God		$20.00	
	Acquiring a High View of the Church		$20.00	
	The Agreement (Unlocking the Favor of God)	$25.00		

NAME		SUBTOTAL	
ADDRESS		DISCOUNT	
CITY/STATE/ZIP		SHIPPING $1.50 MIN.	
MC/VISA/AMER. EXPRESS #	EXP.		
SIGNATURE		TOTAL	

MAIL TO: POWER CHURCH P.O. BOX 200367-ARLINGTON, TX 76006
PHONE: 972-336-0222 FAX: 972-641-7374 EMAIL: APOWERCHURCH@AOL.COM